Cybersafe Young Children

Cybersafe
Young Children

Teaching Internet Safety and Responsibility, K–3

BARBARA SPRUNG
MERLE FROSCHL
NANCY GROPPER

Foreword by Michelle Ciulla Lipkin

TEACHERS COLLEGE PRESS

TEACHERS COLLEGE | COLUMBIA UNIVERSITY
NEW YORK AND LONDON

Published by Teachers College Press,® 1234 Amsterdam Avenue, New York, NY 10027

Cover design by adam b. bohannon.
Cover photo by Dean Mitchell Photography / iStock by Getty Images.
Permissions credit lines appear in Part III and in Appendixes A, B, and C.

Library of Congress Cataloging-in-Publication Data

Names: Sprung, Barbara, author. | Froschl, Merle, author. | Gropper, Nancy, author.
Title: Cybersafe young children : teaching Internet safety and responsibility, K-3 / Barbara Sprung, Merle Froschl, Nancy Gropper ; foreword by Michelle Ciulla Lipkin.
Description: New York, NY : Teachers College Press, 2020. | Includes bibliographical references and index.
Identifiers: LCCN 2019054478 (print) | LCCN 2019054479 (ebook) | ISBN 9780807763742 (paperback) | ISBN 9780807763759 (hardcover) | ISBN 9780807778494 (ebook)
Subjects: LCSH: Internet in education. | Internet and children. | Internet—Safety measures.
Classification: LCC LB1044.87 .S67 2020 (print) | LCC LB1044.87 (ebook) | DDC 371.33/44678—dc23
LC record available at https://lccn.loc.gov/2019054478
LC ebook record available at https://lccn.loc.gov/2019054479

ISBN 978-0-8077-6374-2 (paper)
ISBN 978-0-8077-6375-9 (hardcover)
ISBN 978-0-8077-7849-4 (ebook)

Printed on acid-free paper
Manufactured in the United States of America

Contents

PART IV: RESOURCES

Foreword

Adults have a responsibility to protect and empower children—to protect them in a way that helps them develop the skills they need to ultimately protect themselves as they grow—and to help children learn to ask questions and think critically about the technologies and media they use.

—Joint Position Statement: NAEYC and the
Fred Rogers Center for Early Learning and Children's Media

When my son was around 4 years old, I was speaking with my sister on the telephone discussing my son's obsession with apple juice. I remember complaining about how much juice he was drinking. He asked for it all the time, and I was getting concerned with the amount of sugar he was consuming. My sister responded by asking, "Why don't you stop buying it?" I paused, completely stunned. Here's the thing. This had NEVER occurred to me. Not once. I had started diluting it. I had told him only at mealtimes. I had tried limits, but I never ever thought to stop buying it. I laughed because it was unbelievably obvious and yet it wasn't something that had ever come to my mind. Sometimes the answer is right in front of us, and we look right past it.

I bring this up because I notice this type of experience all the time with parents of young children when they talk about their children's technology use. As a media literacy educator, I am often asked to speak to parents who have concerns about their kids and technology. I was in a session once where a young mom was lamenting about how her son had started to read and how he had started to read her texts. She said, "Sometimes the texts are inappropriate and I don't want him seeing it. I don't know what to do." My response was simple, "Maybe it's time to stop letting him have your phone until he gets a bit older." She looked at me with complete awe and said, "I'd never thought about that." Sometimes the answer is right in front of us, and we look right past it.

When it comes to technology and kids, especially young ones, the answers are often right in front of us. We know the early years of child development are vital. We know children start using technology early. We know children have access to all types of media. We need to accept that it is never too early to educate children about the digital world around them.

As the executive director of the National Association for Media Literacy Education, I spend every day thinking about how we can better prepare students to succeed in today's media-saturated, participatory culture. I have seen the topic of media literacy and digital citizenship start in college classrooms, move to high school, then to middle school, then to elementary school. We are finally learning that education around media and technology is a lifelong process and not something we can wait to start teaching until a child is "old enough."

If we think of teaching students about technology the way we think about helping them learn to read, we build different possibilities. We start reading to children almost immediately. We share board books with infants and recognize the importance of simply reading, regardless of whether they understand what we are saying. When we think of helping children learn to read, we picture an adult sitting next to a child helping them sound out letters, syllables, and words. We take it step by step. It takes years before they start to master the skill. Then we continue to work with children on complex books and more difficult content.

We don't do this with technology. In a lot of ways, we do the exact opposite. We often hand off the technology without explanation, discussion, and guidance. We think that because a child knows how to swipe or press play that they actually understand technology. We often mistake tech savviness with a greater comprehension. We are then surprised when, as children get older, their activity online becomes risky and problems arise. There have been countless times where I have been asked to come into a school *after* the awful cyberbullying incident. If we aren't educating children and teaching them from the earliest age how to be responsible, productive, and kind digital citizens, what do we think is going to happen when they begin to interact in the digital world?

Cybersafe Young Children: Teaching Internet Safety and Responsibility, K–3 asks the most important question: How do we prepare kids for success? The book builds a strong case for early education around digital citizenship and cyberbullying. It outlines a practical plan for early intervention and skill building. It provides a road map and resources for those who work with and support K–3 students.

As technology becomes a bigger and bigger part of our world, we must do whatever we can to provide the next generation with the tools they need and the guidance they deserve. We must support the educators who teach this generation of children with resources like the book you hold in your hands. Education is key. There is no other way. Sometimes the answer is right in front of us, and we can't afford to look past it any longer.

—Michelle Ciulla Lipkin,
Executive Director, National Association for Media Literacy Education

Acknowledgments

Cybersafe Young Children: Teaching Internet Safety and Responsibility, K–3 grew out of Right from the Start in the Digital Age, a national initiative of international nonprofit FHI 360 to help children gain the skills they need to enter the digital world safely and responsibly.

We want to express our deepest appreciation to the funders who provided support for that effort: the Free to Be You and Me Foundation that underwrote the foundational study that informed the project, and the FHI 360 Catalyst Fund that funded the development and launch of the national initiative.

We thank the contributors who gave generously of their time for interviews during the foundational study: Marge Keiser, Parent Coordinator, PS 321, Brooklyn, NY; Michelle Ciulla Lipkin, Executive Director, National Association for Media Literacy Education (NAMLE); Liz Phillips, Principal, PS 321, Brooklyn, NY; Ayelet Segal, Parent, Bank Street School for Children; Lori Skopp, Principal, Abraham Joshua Heschel Middle School; and Alexis Wright, Dean of Children's Programs, Bank Street School for Children.

On March 20, 2015, FHI 360 held an Expert Convening at its New York office to further develop ideas for Right from the Start. The contributions of the participants were invaluable in shaping its content as well as the initiative that was conceived at the meeting. We extend our deepest appreciation to: Kathy Charner, Editor-in-Chief, Books and Related Resources, National Association for the Education of Young Children (NAEYC); Shayna Cook, Program Associate, New America; Chip Donohue, Founding Director, TEC Center, Erikson Institute; Ed Greene, Vice President, Children, Youth and Media Literacy, Hispanic Information Television Network; Michelle Ciulla Lipkin, Executive Director, NAMLE; and Liz Phillips, Principal, PS 321, Brooklyn, NY.

A special thank-you goes to Ed Greene, a longtime supporter of our work to reduce teasing and bullying behavior by creating school cultures focused on building positive social–emotional skills, kindness, and empathy in early childhood settings. He suggested the idea of an Expert Convening to bring national attention to early digital citizenship. Another special thank-you is extended to Michelle Ciulla Lipkin, who brought our ideas to her constituents by creating a place for us at the biannual NAMLE conference devoted to media literacy.

    We also want to thank Liz Phillips who, as principal of PS 321, joins with teachers and parents to help children become good digital citizens. We thank her, and computer teacher Sara Silver, for sharing their work with us.

    Finally, we want to thank Sarah Biondello, our editor at Teachers College Press, who saw the importance of starting good digital citizenship in early education and published this book for the benefit of teachers everywhere. Her support brought our vision to reality. And our deep appreciation goes to Gretchen Adams, who helped us prepare the manuscript for publication.

Preface

PURPOSE

The purpose of this book is to provide background information and best practices for teachers in K–3 classrooms to use as they embed good digital citizenship into the daily life of the classroom. Adding good digital citizenship to the school life of young children can present a challenge for teaching and learning. We offer an educational paradigm that will enable teachers and parents to help young children develop the skills and principles needed to thrive in both the real and the digital worlds in which they live.

BACKGROUND

The authors of this book have spent many years helping teachers of children in grades K–3 address face-to-face teasing and bullying behavior in educationally appropriate ways. We have created evidence-based curricula, provided professional development and parent education, and vetted literacy-based classroom resources that are free of bias due to gender, race/ethnicity, disability, family income, sexual orientation, or gender identity. Our approach, rooted in principles of child development with a strong focus on social–emotional development, encompasses research, practical classroom strategies, and user-friendly curricular activities. With this book, *Cybersafe Young Children: Teaching Internet Safety and Responsibility, K–3*, we bring this comprehensive approach to the issue of young children's safe and responsible participation in the digital world.

As early childhood educators, we are well aware that many children enter school already adept at using digital media. They can swipe, they can access FaceTime, and they can use tablets, computers, smartphones, and apps to play games individually or with friends, all with ease. It is clear that the use of digital media has shaped and will continue to shape the world of young children (Alper, 2011; Flewett, 2011; Linebarger, Piotrowski, & Lapierre, 2009).

This shift, however, has both positive and negative aspects. On the positive side, digital media tools can be harnessed for learning and development

(Donohue, 2015; Guernsey, 2014; NAEYC and the Fred Rogers Center for Early Learning and Children's Media at Saint Vincent College, 2012). They can also promote new skills, raise achievement, and bring children together across time and space (Gutnick, Robb, Takeuchi, & Kotler, 2010).

On the negative side, without guidance children's use of digital media may be inappropriate and can even be dangerous. Although young children may physically know how to swipe a screen or tap an icon, this does not mean that they are prepared to use such devices in safe and responsible ways or that they understand the possible repercussions of such use. Research and the popular press have made it clear that disastrous negative side effects such as cyberbullying can result from inappropriate online behavior. A text message, a Facebook comment, or an Instagram post can lead to devastating consequences, and children in grades K–3 do not yet understand abstract concepts such as privacy and permanence, which are critical to online safety.

TECHNOLOGY AND YOUNG CHILDREN

We recognize that the reader may be questioning the value of delving into young children's use of technology because direct experience and interaction with the world of people and objects is so highly valued in the field of early childhood education. But within that field sensibilities regarding young children's use of technology have evolved since the time that personal computers were first introduced into homes and schools. Initially, there was concern that computer use would take essential time away from the direct, hands-on experiences that young children need in order to develop and learn. Over the decades, attitudes have changed as new interactive technologies and apps have been developed and research on their use has expanded. There is increased recognition that, when used appropriately, a range of technologies can help to promote young children's learning as long as usage is supervised by adults and does not replace their direct experiences with the physical and the social world.

The question is no longer whether or not but *when* and *how* to best use technology as an adjunct to hands-on experience that will foster learning at home and school. The joint position of the NAEYC and the Fred Rogers Center for Early Learning and Children's Media at Saint Vincent College (2012) offers an extensive summary of research on the impact of technology on young children, followed by a set of well-articulated principles regarding its use. We concentrate on two of these principles that are particularly salient to the issue of combating cyberbullying. The first states that "professional judgment is required to determine if and when a specific use of technology or media is age appropriate, individually appropriate, and culturally and linguistically appropriate" and that educators must carefully plan, implement, and evaluate its appropriate educational use in the classroom (p. 6). The second principle asserts that "digital citizenship is an important part of digital literacy for young children" and that it is the role of "adults to help children develop an emerging understanding of the use, misuse, and abuse of technology and the norms of appropriate, responsible, and ethical behaviors related to online rights, roles, identity, safety, security, and communication" (p. 10).

In a 2016 publication, *Early Learning and Educational Technology Policy,* the U.S. Department of Education provides a set of guiding principles to follow when using technology with young children. One principle states that "technology is more effective for learning when adults and peers interact or co-view with young children" (p. 7). This principle provides a segue into the premise of this book. We now know that young children have access to interactive technology and are becoming increasingly adept at using home devices from an early age. Yet supervision at home varies, and even with teachers actively monitoring the use of technology in the classroom, children have become adept at surreptitiously using Facebook, Twitter, and text messaging to communicate with friends on school premises, and we know that such social media activities are used to cyberbully.

Although the phenomenon of cyberbullying typically occurs among older children, face-to-face teasing and bullying already are realities at the early childhood level, and evidence exists that taking a proactive approach serves to reduce its prevalence (Gropper & Froschl, 2000). It follows that it is imperative for educators and parents to take a proactive stance to prevent cyberbullying before it takes hold as a pernicious mode of social interaction, particularly when increased use of interactive technology makes it likely that younger children will become the targets and even the perpetrators.

WHAT YOU WILL FIND IN THIS BOOK

The introduction to *Cybersafe Young Children: Teaching Internet Safety and Responsibility, K–3* offers definitions of cyberbullying and digital citizenship—two important aspects of computer usage that are the foundation for all that follow. This section also contains "The Case for Starting Early," our rationale for creating a classroom culture of kindness and friendship as a means of preventing later cyberbullying. The focus is on developmental and experiential learning as well as the importance of proactive social–emotional development and how to foster positive social interactions among children. The book is then divided into four main sections: Premise, Practice, Classroom Activities, and Resources. Also included is a complete list of references and appendices containing a school statement, parent letters, a questionnaire, and a glossary.

Part I: Premise. Interwoven throughout *Part I: Premise* are issues of gender, relational aggression/bystanders, and social–emotional development. This section contains an overview of national and international research on issues related to children's use of the Internet, including research on children ages 9–18, the ages most studied, and newer research on children in pre-K–grade 3. The section also addresses the critical issue of bystander behavior and looks at cyberbullying prevention through a lens of children's self-awareness, self-management, social awareness, relationship skills, and responsible decision making—all components of positive social–emotional behavior as defined by The Collaborative for Academic, Social, and Emotional Learning (CASEL) and many others. Teachers of children in grades K–3 play a key role in helping their young students develop these critical skills and use them in their daily interactions—face-to-face and online. At the end of Part I, we provide a list of appropriate and helpful recommended readings.

Part II: Practice. *Practice* begins with "Implications for Teacher Education," urging teacher educators and school leadership faculty to include opportunities at the preservice or in-service level to delve more deeply into the issue of cybersafety and good digital citizenship. Also included is a "Message for Teachers and Administrators," which focuses on the importance of a whole-school approach and of integrating lessons about cybersafety and good digital citizenship into the K–3 curriculum as a deterrent to later harmful acts such as cyberbullying. The message acknowledges the broad range of children's experiences with digital media and urges teachers to use their own judgment about how and when to introduce activities into their classroom.

The message is followed by "A Curriculum Map for Good Digital Citizenship," offering suggestions for embedding digital citizenship activities within the context of the classroom throughout the year. The curriculum map urges teachers to assess children's experiences with digital media at the beginning of the school year by asking parents, former teachers, computer lab teachers, and the children themselves about how familiar children are with digital devices and their uses.

The curriculum map also suggests that teachers employ the tried-and-true method of observing children's play and social interactions to learn about how they incorporate digital play into their imaginative scenarios, and it reminds teachers that the beginning of the school year is a good time to conduct activities and establish rules to address face-to-face bullying, particularly at the kindergarten level when children typically do not have the writing skills to engage in cyberbullying. The curriculum map reminds teachers to seek out available guidelines and curricula that address face-to-face bullying at the early childhood level. These resources can serve as a base for creating a prosocial classroom climate that fosters friendship and empathy and that recognizes the harmful effects of teasing and bullying behavior, including the role of bystanders. Recognizing face-to-face events in grades K–3 can serve as a good segue to addressing cyberbullying. Many of these resources appear in the annotated Resources section in Part IV of this guide. This section closes with a descriptive guide to the activities that follow in Part III. The Curriculum Map for Good Digital Citizenship also appears as a chart (see Figure 7.1).

Part III: Classroom Activities. This section contains a series of activities developed by the authors and based on extensive experience in addressing both face-to-face and online bullying in grades K–3. The activities take a developmental approach, with emphasis on building a classroom culture that fosters kindness, empathy, and friendship. Activities are built around essentials of early learning—social–emotional development, literacy, executive function, and conceptual development. Teaching strategies include stories and discussion, role-playing, partnering with older students who will serve as role models, building Internet vocabulary, and problem-solving vignettes. Concepts related to responsible online behavior, such as privacy and permanence, and to "doing the right thing" are addressed. Suggestions for carrying out activities online are included throughout the section.

Activities include:

1. Discovering What We Know—A way for teachers to assess the level of digital experiences children bring with them into the classroom;
2. Creating Rules for Good Digital Citizenship—A funny story to start a discussion about establishing classroom/school rules for online behavior;
3. Word Webs and Charts—A number of ways to build vocabulary for good citizenship;
4. Doing the Right Thing: A Form of Courage—A classic picture book about face-to-face bullying expands into activities about cyberbullying and the role of bystanders;
5. What Does Permanent Mean? A Word Experiment—A concrete example leads children to understand that what they put online stays there;
6. Understanding Privacy: An Important Concept for Online Activities—A message in a sealed envelope demonstrates how to be private and a vignette illustrates how privacy can be breached;
7. Building Good Digital Citizenship—A selection of fun activities conducted while learning from older children how to be good online citizens;
8. Working with Partners—A pairing with upper-grade students is a learning experience for all.

Part IV: Resources. Picture books and early-reader chapter books are an important resource for building literacy, social–emotional strength, empathy, and conceptual development. In choosing material for the classroom library, teachers are urged to keep in mind the large body of children's literature that addresses face-to-face teasing and bullying. This annotated list includes many books about face-to-face teasing and bullying as well as books specific to cyberbullying. Books in the selection depict children from diverse racial and ethnic groups and are free of bias due to gender, disability, and level of family income.

This section also contains an annotated list of national organizations that provide resources for combating both face-to-face bullying and cyberbullying. There are listings for well-known early childhood resources, such as NAEYC, that provide policy statements, suggestions for apps, and myriad other resources for early childhood professionals.

Organizations like Common Sense Media provide curricula, app reviews, and information specific to good digital citizenship for children in pre-K–12. Many of the organizations listed specialize in social–emotional development, which is critical in creating school environments that promote prosocial behavior and mitigate face-to-face teasing and cyberbullying. Some listings are for organizations that focus on technology in early childhood education, such as the Joan Ganz Cooney Center at Sesame Workshop and the Children and Technology Center (TEC) at the Erikson Institute. In addition, many of the national organizations listed provide books, blog posts, fact sheets, and other resources for teachers, schools, and parents to help children learn how to navigate the digital world and social media safely and responsibly. The section also urges teachers in grades K–3 to look to computer lab teachers, local children's librarians, and school librarians as important resources for providing high-quality materials such as curricula, apps, picture books, and chapter books that address face-to-face teasing and cyberbullying in developmentally appropriate ways.

Introduction

Countless generations of children have experienced face-to-face teasing and bullying within and outside of schools, but it is only recently that legislative efforts to combat the problem have taken hold. In the United States, educational responses at the federal level have come through the Office of Civil Rights and the U.S. Department of Education, specifically in regard to harassment on the basis of gender in 2011 and on the basis of disability in 2013. State governments have been more aggressive. According to Cornell and Limber (2016), "By 2015, every state had passed a law that directs school districts or individual schools to develop policies to address bullying. Some of the most common provisions include investigation and reporting of bullying, disciplinary actions for students involved in bullying, staff training and prevention efforts," but laws vary considerably from state to state in these regards and in regard to providing counseling to those involved.

With increasing availability of all manner of social media, cyberbullying has become a variant of bullying that is a matter of growing concern. A white paper issued in 2017 by the Committee for Children, a nonprofit organization that provides research-based programs focusing on social–emotional learning (SEL) development, clearly defines cyberbullying as an area that needs to be addressed comprehensively:

> Cyberbullying is bullying that takes place using electronic technology. A person who bullies or cyberbullies inflicts or intends to inflict harm on the bullying victim. (p. 1)

The committee recommends that school districts select and implement evidence-based SEL and bullying prevention programs that foster positive school climate; set policies, standards, and best practices for both in-school and out-of-school programs; provide training for teachers and other school staff; and apply state/national laws to the problem. The committee, which is recognized for its work in preventing face-to-face bullying, highlights the fact that although every child is susceptible, youth identified as LGBTQ, youth with disabilities, and youth perceived as immigrants or refugees are particularly vulnerable to bullying and cyberbullying. Another susceptible group consists of youth who are disconnected, socially isolated, excluded, or who lack friends.

In citing the impact of cyberbullying, the Committee for Children states:

> Cyberbullying differs from traditional bullying in that perpetrators are physically removed from their victims and from the direct impact of their actions. There may be a greater power imbalance in cyberbullying—perpetrators can anonymously spread messages to large audiences very quickly, and cyberbullying can take place 24 hours a day, is unsupervised, and is not limited to school hours. As a result, cyberbullying may have more of an effect on a child's emotional health than traditional bullying alone. With youth culture largely focused on social media and digital interactions, children may find it extremely difficult to disengage from technology even when it is a source of bullying. (Committee for Children, 2017, p. 3)

As is the case with face-to-face bullying, state education legislation in regard to cyberbullying varies, but by 2010 a total of 34 states had adopted legislation to address the issue (National Council of State Legislatures, 2010).

Although there are substantial efforts to combat cyberbullying in middle and high schools, there is far less focus on the issue at the elementary school level, particularly in grades K–3.

THE CASE FOR STARTING EARLY

Early childhood educators are well aware that the rapid shift to digital media is reshaping the world of even the youngest children. Well before many children are enrolled in any type of formal educational setting, the use of cell phones, tablets, and other digital devices are an integral part of daily life. Thirty-eight percent of children under the age of 2 are now using smartphones, tablets, and e-readers at the same rates children 8 and under were 2 years ago (Common Sense Media, 2013). By grade 3, some 18% to 20% of children report that they have their own cellphones (Englander, 2011), and by 2013, mobile media usage among 5-to-8-year-olds rose from 52% to 83% (Common Sense Media, 2013).

When 2-year-olds are "expert" at swiping a smartphone to bring up pictures of family members or a favorite television character, 2nd-graders can make Microsoft PowerPoint presentations, and children in kindergarten through grade 3 are playing interactive games online with friends and visiting extended family on FaceTime and Skype, it is a safe assumption that communicating digitally is the "norm." This norm presents the field of early childhood education with a new challenge for teaching and learning: how to develop good digital citizenship at the earliest levels of education. Digital citizenship, which has been defined as the norms of appropriate, responsible behavior with regard to technology use, becomes an essential skill that children need to use the Internet in responsible ways, to keep them safe online, and to prevent and protect them from harmful behaviors such as cyberbullying. A major reason to start early is to avoid the need to remediate negative online behavior when children start using the Internet more independently in 4th or 5th grade.

To date, efforts to create responsible online behavior and prevent cyberbullying have focused mostly on students in middle school and above. However, as the age that children become engaged in the digital world escalates downward, so must research and programmatic efforts be undertaken to help them learn how to navigate online in safe and responsible ways. Developing and guiding children's online activities in the K–3 classroom requires new avenues of professional development for teachers. Teachers will first need to understand several aspects of online communication and then translate that understanding into developmentally appropriate curriculum for children in grades K–3. Issues to be considered include online cybersafety, cyberbullying, social behavior, and social–emotional skills related to online interactions.

The prevention of harmful behaviors such as cyberbullying is one essential reason for starting early. Cybersafety, defined as the safe and responsible use of information and communication technologies, is another. Research conducted in Australia strongly supports the need to start early. In an article, "Cybersafety in Early Childhood Education," Anne Grey (2011) states, "As soon as young children begin to engage with cyber technologies, they should begin cybersafety education" (p. 77). Grey also points out that, in addition to building cybersafety into the early childhood curriculum, starting early provides opportunities to create new and exciting avenues for teaching and learning.

Developing cybersafety skills in early childhood requires teachers and other community members who care for children to revisit and rethink what they have done in the past. In an article titled "Developing Thoughtful Cybercitizens," Michael and Ilene Berson (2004) raise the point that, for real-world safety, children are taught to know how to identify themselves and how to provide their name, address, and telephone number. For online purposes, however, it is essential that children understand to *never* reveal their identity and that their password is not something to be shared, even with a best friend. Cybersafety also brings into play issues of privacy and permanence, abstract concepts that are usually not part of early education and that present curricular challenges to teachers of young children.

It takes creative thinking to develop activities that inform children about online safety and good digital citizenship while allowing them to take full advantage of the opportunities for global outreach and access to information that the Internet provides. One study summarizes key steps that schools and teachers should undertake:

- promote the positive, safe, and effective use of technology;
- integrate online safety awareness;
- ensure the provision of information and communication technology and digital skills for teachers, supported by awareness-raising about risks and safety for young people online;
- develop whole-school policies regarding possible uses as well as protocols to deal with instances of online bullying and harassment; and
- form partnerships and sources in the delivery of Internet safety and education. (Livingstone, Haddon, Gorzig, & Olafsson, 2010, p. 33)

Although teachers are being asked to incorporate many new facets of good digital citizenship into their daily schedule, they do not have to be digital experts to do so. Most important is that the intentional planning that goes into a trusting, respectful learning environment where children feel comfortable and welcome needs to extend to online activities—and it all needs to begin at the earliest levels of education.

Ample evidence supports starting early to develop digital citizenship, a term used to express how adults and children can be responsible digital citizens through an understanding of the use, abuse, and misuse of technology as well as the norms of appropriate, responsible, and ethical behaviors related to online rights, roles, identity, safety, security, and communication (NAEYC, 2012). Classic long-term research, such as the Perry Preschool Project, suggests that starting sooner rather than later will help children develop a strong sense of knowing right from wrong (Schweinhart, Barnes, & Weikart, 1993). It is reasonable to assume that starting early also will help children transfer their understanding of right from wrong to the digital world.

A FOCUS ON DEVELOPMENT
AND EXPERIENTIAL LEARNING IN GRADES K–3

Although clear evidence exists that increasingly even preschoolers have access to social media, we have chosen to focus on children in grades K–3. By the age of 5, most children are cognizant of others as separate from themselves and more aware that the feelings of others are not just a mirror of their own.

Furthermore, they are at the cusp of developing an internalized sense of right and wrong. According to noted moral development theorist Lawrence Kohlberg, at age 5 children typically act in terms of their own interests and needs and let others do the same. But with gradual maturation and experience during the years from 5 to 8, they increasingly want to meet the expectations of others, and they become more invested in seeing themselves as good and being seen as good by others (Lightfoot, Cole, & Cole, 2018).

This is, therefore, a prime time of life to explore what it means to be a friend to others in the classroom and in the school and to directly discuss the phenomenon of bullying. It follows that it is also a time to extend children's understanding of good citizenship as it applies to the cyberworld.

We know that the individual outside-of-school experiences of K–3 children vary greatly. Undoubtedly, many students have ready access to smartphones and tablets, whereas others have little or no access. Because young children learn through direct experience, it would be premature to launch into a cyberbullying prevention program without first considering children's prior experience with social media and with explicit curricula designed to address face-to-face teasing and bullying.

An experiential approach is therefore called for—one in which concepts related to face-to-face teasing and bullying are first introduced, ideally in kindergarten, within the context of what it means to be a good classroom and school citizen. We urge educators to start there.

In keeping with an experiential approach, we believe it is also critical to ascertain what kinds of exposure to social media children have had outside of school. Many parents share the concerns of educators regarding the phenomenon of cyberbullying and can be invited to provide information about their children's prior social media exposure if it is solicited with the expressed purpose of a plan to work with their children over time so that they become good digital citizens before they are likely to encounter cyberbullying.

Part I

PREMISE

CHAPTER 1

What the Research Tells Us

Preteens and Teenagers in the Digital Age

The research confirms what we know empirically from observation and experience. Preteens and teenagers, having grown up in a digital world, are adept at using the Internet for schoolwork and entertainment, and for communicating with one another on a variety of social media platforms.

Internationally, researchers have devoted substantial resources to investigating the effects of the exponential rise of digital technology among youth ages 9–18. The majority of the studies have used surveys to tap into the way preteens and teenagers use digital devices, the positive aspects of being online, and what, if any, their fears are about online communication. For example, EU-Kids Online, a 2010 study of over 25,000 European children ages 9–16, documented that children in 25 countries across the continent were already thoroughly embedded online. In 2010, a total of 93% reported being online at least weekly and 60% daily. Fifty-nine percent were on social networks, and 26% had a public profile. Children reported being exposed to injurious messages—for example, about self-harm, drug-taking, and anorexia. Thirty percent of children reported that excessive use of the Internet led to less time for friendship, lack of sleep, and neglect of schoolwork (Livingstone et al., 2010).

At the time of the study, students reported that face-to-face bullying was more of a problem than online bullying. Since then, however, in many studies students attest to the fact that cyberbullying is the downside of their online lives.

In a 2016 study conducted by the Cyberbullying Research Center (Patchin, 2016) involving almost 6,000 students, it was documented that over 30% of students ages 12–17 report that they experienced cyberbullying. The study surveyed a nationally representative sample of middle and high school students. Incidents experienced by students ranged from receiving mean/hurtful comments (22.5%), receiving cellphone threats (11.9%), posting racist comments (10%), or posting mean/hurtful videos (7.4%).

A study conducted in 2018 by the Pew Research Center also documents far more online bullying and harassment. The report, based on telephone and online surveys with 1,058 parents and 743 teenagers, found that 42% of teens experienced offensive name-calling, 32% were victims of false rumors, 25% received explicit messages that they didn't ask for, 16% received physical threats, and 7% had explicit images of them shared online without consent. Ninety percent of teens believed that online harassment is a problem. Six in 10 parents worried that their own teen would be bullied online. Interestingly, a majority of teens stated that parents do a good job protecting them but were critical of teachers, social media sites, and the responses of politicians to the problem of online bullying and harassment (Anderson, 2018).

Nationally and internationally, educators know that cyberbullying prevention is a must. Teaching and learning about digital citizenship, responsible online behavior, and cybersafety has become an essential part of the curriculum, presenting a new challenge and paradigm for teachers.

GENDER CONCERNS

Data from the Cyberbullying Research Center (2016) reveals that girls experience more cyberbullying (36.7%) than boys (30.5%). The Pew research mentioned previously documents that girls and boys experience online bullying differently. The Pew study shows that, typically, girls are subjected to mean remarks, the spreading of false rumors, and the posting of unwanted or sexualized messages/photos online. Boys are subjected to online name-calling and physical threats. These gender differences parallel the ways in which girls and boys experience face-to-face bullying and harassment (Anderson, 2018, p. 4).

A study conducted by researchers at Simon Fraser University in British Columbia, Canada, describes gender differences in cyberbullying through the lens of relational aggression. Titled "you were born ugly and youl [sic] die ugly too," the 2-year study specifically focused on whether girls were more likely to use relational aggression strategies for cyberbullying (Jackson, Cassidy, & Brown, 2009). Three hundred sixty-five students in grades 6–9 from diverse socioeconomic and racial backgrounds completed a 40-minute survey, including closed and open-ended questions related to cyberbullying. The age group was selected because middle school is when cyberbullying is prevalent. Although a majority of students self-reported that they had not been subjected to cyberbullying, those who had been victimized showed that more girls than boys (16% vs. 11%) reported receiving sexual insinuations through text messages and that many more girls than boys received messages that made them feel afraid (12.6% vs. 8.7%). More than twice as many girls reported that they received messages that threatened their reputation (17 girls, 8 boys), and almost twice as many girls said that negative messages affected their ability to concentrate on schoolwork (12 girls, 7 boys) and their ability to make friends (13 girls, 7 boys).

In summary, throughout most of the questions on the survey, more girls than boys felt threatened by others, isolated from peers, and unable to concentrate on schoolwork, and more girls expressed a desire to perpetrate cyberbullying as a response. Almost twice as many girls have been harassed because of gender (16.3% vs. 8.1%); 29% of boys and 20% of girls reported receiving messages labeling them gay or lesbian, even if they are not. Interestingly, though the terms "gay" and "lesbian" are used as pejoratives in cyberbullying, students reported that those who had "come out" were not likely to be cyberbullied because of it. As in face-to-face bullying, victims of cyberbullying were individuals with mental and/or physical disabilities, unfashionable clothes, unusual body compositions, abnormal academic or athletic abilities, and/or the "nerds" and "geeks."

Another interesting gender finding of the study concerned role-playing online. More boys than girls pretended to be older online so that they could access adult websites, or they assumed a different personality. Girls' role-playing involved pretending to be a different age and to counterfeit physical appearance. The authors of the study conclude that gender is an important factor in examining cyberbullying in the context of relational aggression—for example, gossiping, talking behind someone's back, or using put-downs. According to their findings, "girls are more covert and intend, when bullying, to harm friendships and exclude through isolation; boys engage more often in the physical form of bullying" (Jackson et al., 2009, p. 77).

Sexting, defined as "sending and receiving of sexually explicit or sexually suggestive images or video via a cellphone," is another important gender concern (Hinduja & Patchin, 2010, p. 1). In 2010, the Cyberbullying Research Center surveyed approximately 4,400 randomly selected students, ages 11–18, from a large public-school district. Males sent and received more sexually explicit photos than females (8.1% sent and 15.9% received vs. 7.2% sent and 9.9% received). The peak age for sexting is 14–16, understandable in terms of puberty and hormonal development. The researchers caution against overreacting to teenage sexting and urge educators to develop age-appropriate strategies to keep students safe. For girls, sexting has greater consequences than for boys. In many instances, girls send a sexual image of themselves to a boy they care about, only to have it shared with others, resulting in being called a "slut" or a "whore." In extreme cases, sexting has led to teenage girls committing suicide (Hinduja & Patchin, 2010, p. 1).

Researchers recommend that school districts adopt an anti-sexting policy for students as follows:

- Clearly state that possession of sexually explicit images of minors on any device is prohibited regardless of whether any state laws are violated;

- All individuals involved in sexting, unless the image(s) are immediately deleted, are subject to discipline;
- Students should be notified that their parents and the police may be contacted to investigate;
- Students should be notified that cellphones will be searched if there is reasonable suspicion that the phone contains evidence of violating school policy—for example, contains sexting images; and
- Consequences must be clearly stated, while punishment is decided on a case-by-case basis. (Hinduja & Patchin, 2010, p. 3)

CYBERBULLYING, SELF-HARM, AND SUICIDE

Research also confirms what has been widely reported in the popular press: that, although the Internet can be a positive tool for learning and social communication, it is also a powerful vehicle for cyberbullying with tragic results. For example, a systematic review conducted over 21 years with more than 150,000 European children and youth showed that victims of cyberbullying are twice as likely to self-harm or attempt suicide. The research revealed that perpetrators of cyberbullying also are at higher risk of experiencing suicidal thoughts and behaviors. Professor Ann John, lead author of the study, concludes:

> Suicide prevention and intervention is essential within any comprehensive anti-bullying program and should incorporate a whole-school approach to include awareness training for staff and pupils. (John et al., 2018)

In the United States, shocking reports of suicide carried out by 9- and 12-year-old children who were severely cyberbullied have appeared in the popular press. The research is not extensive, but one study that surveyed a random sample of 1,963 middle school students from one of the largest school districts found that youth who had experienced traditional bullying or cyberbullying, as either offender or victim, had suicidal thoughts or were more likely to attempt suicide. As in the European study, the authors conclude:

> Adolescent peer aggression must be taken seriously both at school and at home, and suggest that a suicide prevention and intervention component is essential within comprehensive bullying response programs implemented in schools. (Hinduja & Patchin, 2010, p. 3)

At the extreme end of harm, according to a survey of students conducted by the Centers for Disease Control and Prevention, 16% of students reported seriously considering suicide, 13% reported creating a plan to do so, and 8% reported trying to take their own life in the year preceding the survey (cdc.gov/healthcommunication/index.html). Because cyberbullying reaches its highest level in middle school, starting early to prevent online cruelty among adolescents is critical.

SUMMARY

This chapter provides background and context for the role that cyberbullying plays in the online lives of youth, ages 9–18. It clearly demonstrates that the harm of face-to-face bullying has migrated to the Internet, with serious and long-term effects on victims. It makes the case that, as in addressing face-to-face bullying, the place to start is in the early childhood years, before children are fully online. Issues of classroom/school climate, gender differences in the ways that cyberbullying plays out, and teacher comfort/education are discussed in the research outlined previously. As educators struggle with how to create best practices for addressing digital citizenship and cyberbullying prevention, the role of social–emotional learning, long a priority in early childhood education, takes on a new importance for older students.

CHAPTER 2

Digital Citizenship and Cybersafety

A Priority Early Education Concern

It is clear from the time they are toddlers that children are swiping smartphones to find pictures of friends and family, having FaceTime visits with grandparents and others, and will soon be using tablets to play games online with friends.

This phenomenon is defining emerging issues for early childhood researchers, teacher educators, and practitioners. The use of digital media in early childhood has grown so rapidly that research on the short- and long-term effects lags behind. Questions about how to ensure cybersafety schoolwide, how to integrate developmentally appropriate curriculum, and how to design effective professional development around digital citizenship for K–3 teachers top the list.

Children in grades K–3 are the focus of this book; what the current research tells us is critical to the development of best practices for teaching cybersafety and digital citizenship. A summary of key studies and articles based on these grades and that speak to the issues discussed previously follows.

In the United States, the Massachusetts Aggression Reduction Center at Bridgewater State University (MARC) conducted a 2-year research study (Englander, 2011) with nearly 12,000 students in 3rd, 4th, and 5th grades. Here is a selection of their findings:

- Over 90% of 3rd-graders reported playing interactive games online;
- Thirty-five percent of 3rd-graders reported owning a cellphone, and cellphone usage increased in every subsequent grade;
- Most elementary cyberbullying occurred during online games;
- Between 2010 and 2012, girls' use of Facebook increased from 19% to 49%;
- In 3rd grade, 72% of children who experienced cyberbullying said that the bully was anonymous. By 5th grade, the percentage dropped to 64%, suggesting the bully and victim knew each other.

Based on their research, MARC has developed a comprehensive K–5 curriculum, including 10 lesson plans for each grade, professional development for teachers, and planned interactions between younger and older

students. The curriculum, which encourages classroom discussion and focuses on the emotional impact of bullying/cyberbullying on victims and bystanders, was evaluated in two schools in Massachusetts, one urban and
one suburban, with large differences in socioeconomic status between the
two. In the urban setting, 55% of children were eligible for free lunch; in
the suburban setting, 2% were similarly eligible. Evaluation of the curriculum reported moderate to high positive impact, with kindergarten children
being less engaged than children in grades 1–5. Evaluation also revealed
that high-quality, experienced teachers felt uncertain about their ability to
teach cyber content (Englander, 2011). The MARC study certainly supports
the rationale for addressing cyberbullying early. In the words of Elizabeth
Englander, director of MARC, "Cyber–education needs to begin well before
middle school."

Internationally, Australia, Britain, and the Scandinavian countries
have been leaders in early childhood research. "Young Children's Everyday
Concepts of the Internet: A Platform for Cyber-Safety Education in the
Early Years," a small, randomized study conducted in Australia, addresses
Internet activity of 4–5-year-olds, with a focus on cybersafety (Edwards et
al., 2018). The study involved 48 children in the trial group and 22 children
in the control group. Four experienced teachers participated, three in the
trial group and one in the control group. The children were of mixed Asian
and Western European cultures from upper-middle-class families. The study
grew out of the awareness and concern on the part of researchers that, because of the ease of using devices such as mobile phones and touchscreen
tablets, children as young as 4–5 years old were able to access the Internet
without adult supervision. The authors of the study use the term "digitods"
to describe the first generation to be fully online from birth.

Although the study involved small numbers of children and teachers,
it is important because its purpose was to investigate how early childhood
teachers can engage young children in cybersafety education in developmentally appropriate ways consistent with accepted principles of child development. Citing the lack of evidence-based cybersafety education, the
researchers wanted to learn more about children's "Internet cognition,"
for example, to establish an exploratory knowledge base about young children's "everyday concepts" of the Internet (Edwards et al., 2018, p. 48).
The study drew on Vygotsky's (1987) ideas about "everyday concepts" and
"scientific concepts" that children use to reach a level of "mature concepts,"
those that are based on reason.

The authors base their ideas about how to teach concepts of cybersafety
to young children on what is known about how children construct knowledge based on experimentation and experience. As children cook food, they
build understanding of the way that heat changes the state of food from raw
to cooked—for example, a chemical change has occurred. Understanding the
"why" of this chemical change is what Vygotsky labels "mature concepts."

The authors posit that, rather than adapting methods used to teach cyber-safety to older children, early childhood educators need to build on children's "everyday concepts" of the Internet as a base on which to foster more mature concepts—in other words, to help children understand the "why" (Edwards et al., 2018).

In an article titled "Digital Play," Edwards (2018) acknowledges that, with the proliferation of touchscreen devices, young children are fully engaged in digital play. She reviews current research that is directed toward theorizing digital play and understanding the convergence of traditional play with technological activity as a form of digital play. Edwards's article has identified some important questions for further research. She asks to what extent digital play builds young children's early science, technology, engineering, and math (STEM) concepts and capabilities; how should parents and educators balance digital play with young children's requirement for active outdoor physical activity; what digital play looks like in an early childhood education and care setting; and whether digital play differs across social, gendered, cultural, and economic contexts according to young children's access to technologies. In discussing implications of young children's digital play for parents, services, and policy, Edwards recommends that young children have access to equal opportunities for digital play and age-appropriate education for digital citizenship (Edwards, 2018).

A qualitative exploratory study across six European countries (Belgium, Czech Republic, Finland, Germany, Italy, and the United Kingdom) and Russia conducted at the Joint Research Centre (Chaudron, Di Gioia, & Gemo, 2015) suggests that young children are no safer online than older children. With the easy use of touchscreens, often without adults nearby, children are exposed to advertisements, pop-ups, or contact with unknown people. The study involved researchers from 10 universities and focused on 70 families. Interviews were conducted with 6- and 7-year-olds who were entering 2nd grade in 2014 and who used digital technology at least once a week, often with an older sibling or a parent. As might be expected, the study revealed that while young children can easily acquire basic operational skills, they had little to no understanding of the Internet or what it means to be "online." Key findings include the following:

- Children are little aware of what the Internet is, what it means to be "online," and what the risks and benefits are.
- Children are "digital natives" (see "digitods," mentioned previously) and are comfortable with basic operational skills. However, they also encounter situations that they cannot manage and need to seek adult or older sibling help.
- In general, 6- and 7-year-old children have limited or no perception of online risks, despite having encountered inappropriate content, pop-ups, and application purchase offers.

- Young children's reading and writing skills influence the quality of their online interactions.
- Parents see digital technology as both positive and challenging— something that needs to be carefully regulated and controlled. Parents would welcome guidance on how to foster online safety.

Although this study focused on digital media activities within the home, many of the recommendations apply equally well to the early childhood classroom. Some salient recommendations are

- developing materials for parents and caregivers that promote critical thinking skills around the use of digital media;
- developing strategies for talking with young children about managing online risks;
- encouraging schools to take a more active role in providing educational uses of technology and addressing online safety; and
- encouraging schools to support the development of teachers' digital skills and their ease in using technology.

The study concludes with a recommendation that families and schools work together to promote digital literacy beginning in kindergarten.

Preschool research conducted in Australia by Anne Grey (2011), a senior lecturer in early childhood education, strongly supports the need to start early. Grey acknowledges that safety issues have always existed as part of early childhood education but that the expanding use of digital devices by young children have added risks not formerly associated with early childhood education. Now, children's use of the Internet has moved safety issues into cyberspace, including concerns about cyberstalking, cyberbullying, online promotion of inappropriate social and health behaviors, exposure to illegal and inappropriate content, and identity theft (Grey, 2011, p. 77). These are serious and unfamiliar issues for early childhood educators. In building cybersafety into the early childhood curriculum, Grey posits that children's use of digital media provides opportunities to create new and exciting avenues for teaching and learning. She suggests using traditional early childhood strategies such as role-playing of hypothetical cybersafety situations through which children can act out appropriate responses, such as clicking a safety button. Other suggestions include posing open-ended questions to develop critical-thinking skills around online messages and materials. Grey's approach to children's entry into the digital world is to integrate safe and responsible online behavior at the earliest level of education. Developing cybersafety skills in early childhood requires teachers and other community members who care for children to revisit and rethink what we have done in the past (Grey, 2011).

In an article titled "Developing Thoughtful Cybercitizens," Michael and Ilene Berson (2004) see social studies curriculum as a way to create "cybercitizenship":

> The connection between responsible choices and global awareness provides a strong linkage between social studies and preparation of students for their role in cyberspace. Cyberspace offers a globally connected community in which elementary school children will be challenged to apply their social competence and ethical decision-making skills within a worldwide forum. (p. 7)

A study by Livingstone et al. (2010) summarizes key steps that schools and teachers should undertake:

1. promote the positive, safe, and effective use of technology;
2. integrate online safety awareness;
3. ensure the provision of Information and Communications Technology (ICT) and digital skills for teachers, supported by awareness-raising about risks and safety for young people online;
4. develop whole-school policies regarding possible uses as well as protocols to deal with instances of online bullying and harassment; and
5. form partnerships and sources in the delivery of Internet safety and education. (p. 33)

SUMMARY

The premise of this book and of an increasing number of early childhood researchers is that if education for digital citizenship begins early, the harm of cyberbullying can be prevented or at least significantly curtailed. Research on both youth and early childhood affirms that teachers must be prepared to integrate digital citizenship into the curriculum and the daily life of the classroom. Whether the term used to describe children's online lives is "digitod," or "cybercitizen," or "digital citizen," the challenge is the same—how to help children develop the skills they will need to be safe and responsible while online.

CHAPTER 3

Cyberbullying Bystanders
Active and Passive Responses

An important, but often overlooked, factor in cyberbullying is the role of bystanders. Bystanders can reinforce or provide support to the bully, they can support and defend the victim, or they can simply remain on the outside of any situation as observers. Although there is ample research on bystander behavior in face-to-face bullying, there is a paucity of research on bystander behavior specifically related to cyberbullying (Allison & Bussey, 2016; Dominguez-Hernandez, Bonell, & Martinez-Gonzalez, 2018; Lenhart, Madden, Smith, Purcell, & Zickuhr, 2011; Olenik-Shemesh, Heiman, & Eden, 2017).

In face-to-face bullying, the bully is known, and the bystanders to the situation, whether active or passive, are also known. With intervention by peers or an adult, it is also possible that there may be face-to-face resolution between the bully and victim or even an apology on the part of the bully and regret from bystanders allied with the bully. In cyberbullying, the fact that the perpetrator can be anonymous, that the online bullying message can (and usually does) become widespread, and that it does not disappear over time makes this behavior even more insidious and dangerous.

Researchers in Spain conducted a systematic review of factors that encourage or hamper young people to intervene in instances of cyberbullying: contextual factors—for example, friendship, social environment, bystander effect, request for assistance, fear of retaliation, and knowledge of effective strategies—and personal factors—for example, individual traits such as empathy, moral disengagement, self-efficacy, previous experience with bullying/cyberbullying, and demographic/socioeconomic data (Dominguez-Hernandez et al., 2018).

Analyzing the contextual factors shows that friendship is critical in determining what kind of bystander action occurs. On the negative side, a good relationship with the bully can favor joining in the bullying, being a passive bystander, or inhibiting another bystander from aiding the victim. On the positive side, group friendship can encourage members to act in support of another member who is being victimized. As a moral issue, friends are expected to stand up for one another. However, it is understood that sometimes, if direct confrontation with the cyberbully is perceived as difficult or even risky, support for friends can be indirect—for example, not taking a public stand, or even going along with the bullying but later providing support privately for the victim.

Regarding personal factors, the research highlights empathy and self-efficacy as important traits in being an active bystander in support of cyberbullying victims. Empathy, the ability to recognize and share in the emotions of someone other than oneself, plays a key role in motivating bystanders to intervene in face-to-face or cyberbullying situations. Self-efficacy, one's sense of one's ability to set and achieve goals, is an important trait that influences one's ability to offer support to a victim of cyberbullying. Interestingly, empathy and self-efficacy are two of the most important characteristics that early childhood educators work to imbue in young children. Therefore, extrapolating these characteristics into an effective cyberbullying curriculum would not seem far out of reach.

The research also identifies moral *disengagement* as a factor in the act of cyberbullying and the negative participation of bystanders. Moral disengagement is defined by social cognitive theory as "the selective or total deactivation of the self-regulatory system that controls moral behavior through specific cognitive mechanisms which legitimate inhumane behaviors" (Bandura, Barbaranelli, Capara, & Pastorelli, 1996, quoted in Dominguez-Hernandez et al., 2018). As expected, research shows that higher levels of moral disengagement lead to negative behaviors on the part of bystanders and serve as a barrier to standing up for cyberbullying victims.

Knowledge of the theory of moral disengagement as a factor in cyberbullying and as a barrier to appropriate intervention by bystanders is important for early childhood educators. Creating curricula activities and a classroom environment that encourages moral *engagement*, along with empathy and self-efficacy, is a strategy for cyberbullying prevention.

Another review, "Cyber-bystanding in Context: A Review of the Literature on Witnesses' Responses to Cyberbullying," looks at cyberbullying as a group phenomenon. While also acknowledging the role of social cognitive theory (see above), this review delineates the "bystander effect" as the dominant paradigm for understanding and explaining bystander inaction (Allison & Bussey, 2016; Dominguez-Hernandez et al., 2018; Lenhart et al., 2011; Olenik-Shemesh et al., 2017).

The bystander effect, described as "the phenomenon whereby individuals are less likely to offer help if other passive bystanders are present" (Allison & Bussey, 2016, p. 184), has been much studied in face-to-face bullying. As components of the effect, bystanders must (1) notice the situation, (2) recognize the need for assistance, (3) feel personally responsible, (4) believe they are able to help, and (5) consciously decide to intervene. Deterrents to intervening are as follows:

- The presence of others may decrease the feeling of personal responsibility.
- Individuals may become self-conscious as others judge their actions.
- Individuals may take the inaction of others to conclude that no action needs to be taken.

Studies to replicate the bystander effect in online cyberbullying have been few, and they have mostly been conducted with adult participants in chat rooms and requests for help sent by email. Awareness of what is known of the bystander effect from real-time studies is needed to inform future research on the role this issue plays in preventing inappropriate cyber-bystander intervention among children.

One study conducted with 1,094 Israeli children and youth (ages 9–18) examined bystander behavior with a focus on active and passive intervention patterns. The researchers looked at how bystanders reacted to cyberbullying incidents in the context of personal aspects, such as age and gender, and socioemotional factors, such as self-efficacy, social support, and sense of loneliness (Olenik-Shemesh et al., 2017).

Among the participants, 46.4% reported being bystanders to cyberbullying; of those, 55.4% did nothing in support of victims, and 44.6% were active participants—for example, helping the victim. However, only 35.6% of bystanders offered direct help after witnessing a cyberbullying event. The researchers also attribute this to the bystander effect described previously. Personal and socioemotional differences played a key role in differences between active and passive bystander behavior. Most interestingly, gender and age were critical factors.

> It was found that the "active bystanders" are most often girls, older, and have more support from significant others, and have lower levels of emotional loneliness than bystanders in the passive group. (Olenik-Shemesh et al., 2017, p. 23)

The researchers suggest that their findings may contribute to developing intervention programs that focus on encouraging children and youth to become more active bystanders—for example, activities for widening the social circle supporting the bystanders through strengthening social networks and peer support, thereby lessening their sense of loneliness and increasing their social confidence.

SUMMARY

Although none of the bystander studies described previously were conducted with children in grades K–3, the results provide strong impetus for educators to be aware that the role of bystander must be addressed at the earliest levels of education. The importance of characteristics such as moral engagement, empathy, and self-efficacy are seen as key factors in active bystander behavior. These are the same characteristics that teachers strive to develop in young children. The research adds to the rationale that cyberbullying prevention, including the role of bystanders, belongs in early childhood.

CHAPTER 4

Preventing Cyberbullying

A Social–Emotional Perspective

A body of evidence exists that situates bullying and cyberbullying within the social–emotional realm. Bullying prevention programs have been proven effective by promoting prosocial behavior such as self-awareness, self-management, social awareness, relationship skills, and responsible decision-making, which are considered essential components of social–emotional learning (SEL) programs (Blatchford, Pelligrini, & Baines, 2016; Ragozzino & Utne O'Brien, 2009). Resilience, self-regulation, empathy, executive function, and moral development have also been identified as important characteristics that can help children resist and combat peer bullying (Hinduja, 2018).

Indeed, empathy serves as a foundation to the development of prosocial and altruistic behavior (Mcdonald & Messinger, 2011). Not only is empathy an antidote to acts of bullying, but, as the previous chapter states, it is a critical factor in the reactions of bystanders. A summary of research on bystander behavior in face-to-face incidents of bullying indicates that bystanders with high levels of empathy are more likely to assume defending roles (Fluke, 2016). But Fluke also asserts that gender plays a role in the reactions of bystanders, pointing to research showing that empathy predicts defending behavior in girls but not in boys. Furthermore, even with high levels of empathy, bystanders may or may not engage in defending behavior depending on who else is present when the bullying occurs. In the case of cyberbullying, the data are even more complicated because bystanders can be and often are invisible. When invisible, they are most likely to be unresponsive to incidents of bullying unless they have some direct connection to the aggressors and/or victims (Jones, 2014). In spite of the complexity of the data in regard to bystanders, it is clearly necessary to address the role and capacity for empathy in any efforts to combat cyberbullying while children are young. Indeed, a summary of research on altruistic behavior indicates that empathy is "a major driving force in prosocial behavior" (Christov-Moore et al., 2014). Furthermore, the authors report evidence from multiple studies that females are more empathic than males. These findings serve to emphasize the value of offering carefully planned educational activities that promote empathy while children are young in order to increase the likelihood of prosocial behavior as they mature.

Most school programs designed to prevent bullying and cyberbullying focus on the middle and high school grades, when students are typically developmentally equipped to evidence social–emotional qualities such as empathy and are, therefore, primed to be receptive to anti-bullying curricula. However, the strength of these capacities among older students is tied to individual rates of maturation and the students' earlier experiences as children at home, in school, and in their communities.

For children in grades K–3, the developmental capacity to evidence these prosocial behaviors is still very much a work in progress. Since early childhood educators do not have direct control of children's experience outside of school, it is up to them to provide in-school experiences that will promote these behaviors within the school setting as an antidote to future bullying and cyberbullying.

SOCIAL-EMOTIONAL PROFILE OF CHILDREN IN K-3

At the early childhood level, learning what it means to be a good digital citizen is an integral part of learning what it means to be an empathic and caring individual who can take others' points of view and respond to the needs of others. By the time children enter kindergarten, they are typically ready to make friends, make comparisons between themselves and others, comprehend the thoughts and feelings of others, engage in cooperative play, distinguish between right and wrong, and listen to others as they speak (Poole, Miller, & Church, 2019). The authors also point out that by the time children are 5 and 6, they are capable of and enjoy sharing their feelings and are better able to read the nonverbal emotional cues of their peers.

When the development of these capacities is supported in positive ways at home and in school, it is more likely that children will become aware of their own feelings, will be able to self-regulate, and will be able to form positive and empathic relationships with peers (Bronson, 2000; Galinsky, 2010). Empathy requires the ability to take the perspective of others, a complex capacity that emerges along with the development of self-awareness and self-regulation. One must be aware of and able to monitor one's own feelings and impulses in order to be able to be sensitive to and respectful of the feelings of others, and this requires the activation of the brain's executive functions that include "inhibitory control, cognitive flexibility, and reflection" (Galinsky, 2010, p. 71). This makes perspective-taking a "truly social–emotional–intellectual skill" (p. 71).

We know that beginning at birth, experience plays an essential role in social–emotional development. Initially it is the family that has the strongest influence on a child's experience, but as the child grows older, other influences come into play. Although it is not within the control of educators to determine children's experience outside of school, educators have an important role to play in shaping children's experience within school in the interests of promoting positive social–emotional and moral development.

EARLY CHILDHOOD PRACTICE
IN SUPPORT OF SOCIAL-EMOTIONAL DEVELOPMENT

Nurturing social–emotional development has been integral to the field of early childhood education since its inception, and literature on the kinds of curricular practices that can accomplish this development is prevalent. For close to a century, early childhood educators have turned to the National Association for the Education of Young Children (NAEYC), originally known as the National Association for Nursery Education, for guidance about sound practice. *Developmentally Appropriate Practice in Early Childhood Programs Serving Children from Birth Through Age 8*, first published in 1987 by NAEYC, is now available in a third edition. It has been used as a resource by generations of teachers and administrators intent on providing a sound educational environment for young children that will promote development within the physical, cognitive, and social–emotional realms (Copple & Bredekamp, 2009).

NAEYC has promoted play as "an important vehicle for developing self-regulation as well as for promoting language, cognition, and social competence" that is closely tied to self-regulation and other social skills (NAEYC, 2009, p. 14). This emphasis on play as the vehicle for promoting social development is shared by the Council for Professional Recognition, the group that published *Essentials for Working with Young Children* (2013, pp. 238–252), which serves as a guide for programs seeking the national Child Development Associate credential.

Whereas these early childhood organizations and their publications are familiar to educators who work with preschool children, they are less familiar to teachers and administrators working with children in grades K–3. Sadly, play has all but disappeared from kindergarten classrooms, and there is no guarantee that children have open-ended play experiences with peers outside of school settings. It is not the purpose of this book to examine how to incorporate play experiences in grades K–3; rather, the reader is encouraged to make use of the organizations and publications cited in this section in order to delve into this in depth to gain greater insight into its value in promoting prosocial behaviors that go hand in hand with preventing bullying and cyberbullying.

THE SOCIAL–EMOTIONAL RISKS
IF CYBERBULLYING IS NOT ADDRESSED

The effects of bullying (and cyberbullying) on victims include physical injury, social problems, emotional problems, and even death. Gender differences have been found in regard to the social–emotional impact of cyberbullying. Girls are more likely to experience emotional problems and boys are more likely to evidence behavioral problems (Soyeon, Scott, Colwell, Boyle, & Georgiades, 2018). Those who bully are also at risk of substance abuse, poor academic performance, and commission of acts of violence as they grow older (National Institutes of Health, 2017). They also suffer such negative consequences as antisocial behavior and suicide as adults. It is particularly noteworthy that one study found that those who are victims of bullying very often engage in acts of bullying. According to Copeland, Wolke, Angold, and Costello (2013), these bully-victims are likely to be aggressive, can be easily angered, and provide support to other bullies. One outcome of this kind of behavior is that peers are less likely to stand up for them. In addition, they are more likely to suffer from depression, anxiety, panic, and suicidal thoughts than those who bully but are not themselves victims.

Even bystanders are at risk. Research on face-to-face bullying indicates that bystanders also experience negative outcomes (Fluke, 2016, pp. 14–15). There is evidence that those who are cyberbullied are also bullied face to face, but cyberbullying poses greater risk because it can invade the victim's life 24 hours a day. Those who are victimized in this way are at risk of damage to their self-esteem, sense of emotional well-being, and academic performance (Cowie, 2013).

SUMMARY

With the risks faced by all involved—bully, victim, bystander—it is a matter of great urgency that we take a proactive stance to combat cyberbullying. Once a context is created in which children in grades K–3 possess a shared language about the meaning and negative impact of teasing and bullying, it is possible to introduce the concept of cyberbullying. It is critical for children to understand what cyberbullying is and how to combat it before they become either victims or aggressors, for if we fail to do so, we put them at serious emotional risk.

Recommended Readings

Allison, K., & Bussey, K. (2016). Cyber-bystanding in context: A review of the literature on witnesses' responses to cyberbullying. *Children and Youth Services Review*, *65*, 13–194.

Berson, M. J., & Berson, I. R. (2004). Developing thoughtful cybercitizens. *Social Studies and the Young Learner*, *16*(4), 5–8. Retrieved from hectorsworld.netsafe .org.nz/wp-content/uploads/cybercitizens-ssyl-2004.pdf

Grey, A. (2011). Cybersafety in early childhood education. *Australasian Journal of Early Childhood*, *36*(2), 77–81.

Hinduja, S. (2018). *Cultivating resilience to prevent bullying and cyberbullying.* Cyberbullying Research Center. Retrieved from cyberbullying.org/cultivating -resilience-prevent-bullying-cyberbullying

Jackson, M., Cassidy, W., & Brown, K. (2009). "you were born ugly and youl die ugly too": Cyber-bullying as relational aggression. *In Education*, *15*(2), 68–82. Retrieved from ineducation.ca/ineducation/article/view/57/538

Nathanson, L., Rivers, S., Flynn, L., & Brackett, M. (2016). Creating emotionally intelligent schools with RULER. *Emotion Review*, *8*(4), 1–6. Retrieved from ei.yale.edu/wp-content/uploads/2016/09/Emotion-Review-2016-Nathanson-1754073916650495.pdf

Ragozzino, K., & Utne O'Brien, M. (2009). *Social and emotional learning and bullying prevention.* Collaborative for Academic, Social, and Emotional Learning School & Social Emotional Learning Group, University of Illinois at Chicago. Retrieved from www.promoteprevent.org/sites/www.promoteprevent.org/files/ resources/SELBullying%281%29.pdf

PRACTICE

CHAPTER 5

Implications for Teacher Education

Education faculty in colleges and universities have an important role to play in preparing teachers and school leaders to combat cyberbullying. Educators must address a range of federal and state requirements in regard to bullying; some also specify cyberbullying. Very often such mandates are met through onetime informational workshops for those seeking professional certification, leaving it up to participants to figure out how to carry this information forward into their practice in schools. Given the severity of negative effects of cyberbullying for victims, bullies, and bystanders, we urge teacher educators and school leadership faculty to include opportunities at the preservice or in-service level for educators and school leaders who work with young children to delve more deeply into the issue of cybersafety and good digital citizenship.

FAMILIARITY WITH FEDERAL AND STATE MANDATES

It is important to first be familiar with existing mandates and how they are fulfilled locally. Do schools and school districts provide staff development workshops or something more comprehensive to help teachers and administrators address cyberbullying? Are such workshops offered by the educational institutions where faculty work? If onetime workshops are the only source of information about this issue for teacher and school leadership candidates, education faculty should seriously consider how to reinforce and supplement the limited information provided in these workshops.

College faculty who prepare teachers and school leaders should also be sure to familiarize themselves with the mandates that exist in their locales in regard to cyberbullying and cybersafety. In the introduction to this book, general information is provided about the nature of federal and state requirements that school districts might have to meet. However, there are wide variations in requirements and how they are met.

An example of a federal mandate is the Children's Internet Protection Act (CIPA), enacted by Congress in 2000 with rules updated by the Federal Communications Commission (FCC) in 2011. This legislation was designed to address a range of concerns about children's Internet safety. However, this legislation applies only to schools and libraries seeking discounts for Internet access or internal connections through what is called the E-Rate Program, which makes certain services and products more affordable. To receive this discount, schools and libraries must adhere to certain requirements, including "provid(ing) for educating minors about appropriate online behavior, including interacting with other individuals or social networking websites and in chat rooms, and cyberbullying awareness and response" (Children's Internet Protection Act, 2011).

An example of how this particular mandate translates into practice at the state level can be seen on the New York State Education Department (NYSED) website. On a page titled Laws and Regulations for Internet Safety and Cyberbullying, reference is made to CIPA legislation, followed by a series of bullets with additional information about state and federal laws that school districts must adhere to, including safeguarding student privacy and complying with New York State's Dignity for All Students Act (DASA), which "prohibits all forms of discrimination or harassment, including cyberbullying" and "also requires instruction in safe and responsible use of the Internet and electronic communications" (New York State Department of Education, 2013). All candidates for teacher and school leader certification in New York State are required to take a DASA workshop at an approved site, and all school leaders must be knowledgeable about the need to comply with state and federal laws in this regard. But the workshops do not provide specificity about how to develop effective programs that not only meet but go beyond the requirements in ensuring that children, particularly those in grades K–3, are being educated in a way that lays a strong foundation for good digital citizenship. In addition, these requirements have little or no bearing on the content of education courses and highlight the need for education faculty to become familiar with relevant regulations as a starting, not a stopping, place for preparing teachers and school leaders to deal with cyberbullying and cybersafety in ways that are appropriate for young children.

INCORPORATING THE ISSUE OF CYBERBULLYING INTO EDUCATION COURSE CONTENT

College faculty can also infuse content about bullying, cyberbullying, cybersafety, and the meaning of good digital citizenship into the courses they teach. We recognize that finding pathways to incorporate additional content into existing academic courses can be challenging. The content included in any given course syllabus must be in keeping with the institution's course catalog description, and all courses typically undergo departmental, institutional, and even state review and approval. Nevertheless, the content of courses is not carved in stone, and college faculty are expected to make changes in order to remain current within the discipline they teach.

Programs that prepare K–3 teachers may be housed in early childhood or elementary education programs, depending on state and local requirements. Still, there is great consistency across programs and institutions in regard to the kinds of courses that teacher candidates are required to take in order to teach those grades. Among these are a number of categories of courses that may lend themselves to addressing the issue of cyberbullying and preparing students to be good digital citizens, including the following:

- applied child development courses,
- courses focused on observing and recording children's behavior,
- educational foundations courses,
- language arts and literacy courses,
- social studies curriculum courses,
- courses focused on the use of technology in the classroom and school, and
- field-based practicums and student teaching courses in which students are required to develop and implement individual activities and integrated unit plans.

For each of these types of courses, reading assignments can include books and articles related to cyberbullying, such as this book in its entirety or parts of the book, as well as other publications that are mentioned here as recommended readings or references.

For example, applied child development courses and courses in which teacher candidates learn to observe and record children's behavior cover topics including social–emotional development, moral development, empathy, and self-regulation. So much of early childhood classroom practice is geared to helping young children contemplate and learn what it means to be a good classroom and school citizen. The Introduction and Part I of this book point out the connection between moral disengagement and bullying, and it follows that preservice teachers should come to recognize that good digital citizenship is an extension of efforts to promote moral development and empathy and will hopefully motivate them to directly address cyberbullying and cybersafety when they have classrooms of their own.

Part II: Practice and Part III: Classroom Activities are relevant to courses focused on teaching language arts and literacy as well as social studies. The suggested activities in Part III can all be used to promote receptive and expressive language skills as well as to foster a sense of what it means to be a positive member of a social community.

Educational foundations courses cover the history of education writ large and typically bring students up to date on legislation that has a direct impact on school practice. It would be prudent to include in these courses an examination of existing legislation that relates to cyberbullying and cybersafety in order to reinforce awareness of the legislative mandates that students in the course will be required to meet as teachers or school leaders.

National accreditation associations such as the Council for the Accreditation of Educator Preparation (CAEP) require teacher and school leader preparation programs in which "candidates model and apply technology standards as they design, implement and assess learning experiences to engage students and improve learning" (CAEP, 2013, Standard 1.5). Many colleges and universities offer educational technology courses to meet this standard and to ensure that their candidates are well versed in the use of educational technology. This is another place appropriate to the infusion of content that helps young children understand the meaning of good digital citizenship and cybersafety.

Courses that include a practicum or fieldwork placement as well as student teaching courses are ideal places to situate content about cybersafety and good digital citizenship. Students who are preparing to be teachers can select activities from Part III of this book or develop comparable alternative activities that address the topic. Student teachers may have the opportunity to deal with this in a more comprehensive way by developing an integrated unit plan with multiple activities focused on the theme of good digital citizenship.

We urge education faculty to find ways to incorporate content about cyberbullying and cybersafety into their own courses, but it is also possible for faculty to take a more systemic approach to achieving this end. Raising the question in faculty meetings of how best to prepare all candidates to combat cyberbullying and promote cybersafety and good digital citizenship can lead to curriculum mapping across coursework programs to ensure that the issue is revisited within a curriculum spiral. This systemic approach can serve as a model for those who enter the education professions for dealing with this complex issue in ways that promote children's learning and conceptual development in a sustained way.

CHAPTER 6

Message for Teachers and Administrators

Cyberbullying is a deeply disturbing phenomenon that has set off alarm bells in middle and high schools where students are frequently victimized. By middle school, students are already deeply immersed in using social media to communicate with friends, and evidence shows that this is when they are most likely to encounter cyberbullying as victims or as bystanders, or worse, as aggressors if no preventive measures are taken. Although the age at which children are initially exposed to cyberbullying may vary, it is clear that even very young children have access to the devices that can serve as a gateway into the world of cyberbullying.

By addressing cyberbullying in grades K–3, educators can lay important groundwork for developing students into good digital citizens in the present and future. We know that children are using digital technology and social media at younger and younger ages. In a small pilot survey of 39 parents conducted by FHI 360 in 2013, most parents of children in grades K–5 in a New York City public school said that their children used some form of digital technology. Eighty-four percent of the parents indicated that their children used computers, 61% indicated that their children used tablets, 42% indicated that their children used cellphones, and 37% indicated that their children used iPads. There was little difference between grade levels for use of all types of technology (FHI 360, 2016).

In a more recent and extensive study that focused on young children, Plowman (2015) found that by the time children start kindergarten at age 5 they have already been exposed to all manner of technological devices, including

> desktop and notebook computers, mobile phones, MP3 players, televisions and game consoles and the products or outputs—such as DVDs, websites, games and interactive stories—that are viewed, read, played or created on these devices. All the children (in this study) also had technology toys, including play laptops or robotic dogs.

In order to counter cyberbullying, researchers recommend a whole-school approach, which has been shown to be most effective in countering face-to-face bullying and teasing. Components of a whole-school approach include professional development for teachers, workshops for nonprofessional staff, workshops for parents, and a written school policy that defines the behavior and consequences (Froschl, Sprung, Mullen-Rindler, Stein, & Gropper, 1998; Olweus, Limber, & Brelvik, 2019; Second Step, 2018).

As an example, at PS 321, an elementary school in Brooklyn, New York, there is a concerted effort to create good digital citizens. The principal sends out a statement to parents at the start of the school year that begins:

> At PS 321, we believe in educating students to be kind, responsible digital citizens and to harness the power of technology for positive uses. We teach all students to code in grades 3–5 and teach students about digital citizenship and safety in all grades. We have a very rich technology program for our upper-grade students. However, over the past few years, we have seen an increase in children's use of various digital devices outside of school (smartphones, tablets, computers, gaming systems) in negative ways. Social networking has become a much bigger part of students' lives at home. As parents navigate the challenges of shaping their children's technology use, we want to share some thoughts and recommendations with you. Although parents of older children probably understand that this handout is relevant to them, we want to urge parents of younger children to take it seriously as well. The earlier parents are aware of some of the potential problems of using digital devices, the easier it will be to avoid or minimize some of the problems.

The statement also outlines school policy: "Smartphones and smartwatches may never be used during the school day at PS 321. They must remain in backpacks at all times, including at lunch and recess (and out-to-lunch)." (For the full statement, see Appendix A.)

The computer teacher at PS 321 also sends a letter asking parents to continue conversations with their children about digital responsibilities and online safety. It suggests questions as well as talking points and resources for parents to help facilitate a meaningful discussion around online behavior, safety, and security. (See Appendix B.) In her classroom she teaches a grades 3–5 Digital Citizenship Unit, which covers topics such as Internet Safety, Privacy and Security, Relationships and Communication, Cyberbullying, Digital Footprint, and Reputation.

Promoting prosocial behavior is already an integral part of the work of early childhood educators. They typically engage their students in establishing classroom rules regarding acceptable social behavior, help them learn to share, foster their appreciation of difference and diversity, engage them in cooperative learning, and facilitate the positive resolution of conflicts. These efforts are designed to create a strong sense of community within and beyond the classroom, and it is not too soon to extend this sense to the digital world. Yet many teachers at the early childhood level do not perceive that social media use and cyberbullying can be incorporated into their efforts to promote prosocial behavior.

To better understand the ways in which social–emotional learning and digital consumption are integrated in early childhood classrooms, Scholastic conducted a survey with prekindergarten through 2nd-grade teachers. Ninety-two percent said that children, even the youngest, were exposed to technology, and nearly 60% said children were exposed to technology in the classroom every day. Yet the vast majority of teachers (95%) said they were not teaching about responsible behavior online. Most indicated that they felt their students were too young or that the materials were not age appropriate. Yet these same teachers rated social and emotional learning as the predominant theme among social development programs already implemented in their schools and early childhood centers with virtually all teachers teaching themes of kindness (Scholastic, Power of Kindness presentation, Power of Zero campaign launch, March 2019 [see the Organizational Resources for information on Power of Zero]). Our underlying assumption is that a proactive, prosocial stance against cyberbullying in grades K–3 will help to prevent incidents of cyberbullying later on and that this effort fits well with current practice in early childhood classrooms where social–emotional learning in general and kindness in particular are emphasized.

Opportunities abound to integrate learning about good digital citizenship into the daily life of the classroom. The curriculum map and embedded activities that we offer are not intended as add-ons that are outside the scope of traditional K–3 curriculum. Rather, they cohere with educational goals of promoting social emotional learning, executive function, literacy development, and conceptual development. Familiar teaching strategies form the basis for activities, including charting, story and discussion, word webs, role-playing, writing, and worksheets. Suggestions are included for conducting activities online for classrooms where whiteboards, tablets, or computers are in use.

The activities that zero in on good digital citizenship presuppose that classroom rules about treating one another with kindness and respect have been established and that the classroom culture supports these rules. It also presupposes that issues about face-to-face teasing and bullying are addressed in an ongoing way through picture books, class meetings, and discussion.

Embedded in the meaning of good digital citizenship are complex concepts about privacy and permanence that may be elusive to young children. However, with thoughtful planning that draws on and expands the experiences children have had with interactive technology, children in grades K–3 can be given direct experience with these concepts. By integrating the meaning of responsible online behavior and good digital citizenship while building a strong sense of community within the classroom, early childhood educators can have a strong impact on the future online citizenship of their young students.

SUMMARY

It is our goal to provide early childhood teachers with a sound approach to address cyberbullying. Even if there is a schoolwide approach to addressing cyberbullying, it is essential to implement activities that are specifically designed for the lower grades (K–3) for all the reasons covered in this book.

If school administrators have not yet adopted a whole-school approach but are interested in doing so, we hope to buoy its integration into the ongoing curriculum in a way that takes into account children's prior experience within and outside of school as the starting point for enacting activities intended to prevent students from becoming future bullies in the digital world. Furthermore, if there is a technology teacher in the school, this person is an excellent resource and collaborator in helping classroom teachers and administrators to implement a curriculum that will be effective.

CHAPTER 7

A Curriculum Map for Good Digital Citizenship

Good digital citizenship is a natural outgrowth of efforts to promote prosocial behavior. This chapter offers a curriculum map for preparing children in grades K–3 to be good digital citizens who will recognize and be prepared to stand up to cyberbullying. It identifies categories of activities within which addressing face-to-face teasing and bullying serves as a precursor to addressing cyberbullying.

Teachers can use the map shown in Figure 7.1 to plan a curriculum that unfolds over part of or throughout the entire school year, integrating activities into the ongoing language and literacy and/or social studies curriculum. Because this book focuses on cyberbullying, no specific plans are offered in regard to the activities about face-to-face teasing and bullying. However, these are important precursors to activities related to cyberbullying, and teachers are encouraged to devise their own activities or to turn to the Internet, where they can find rich resources for developing such activities. Specific activity plans offered here to address cyberbullying can be implemented as written but can also be adapted or supplemented as teachers see fit. The activities in the curriculum map are listed in a suggested sequence that can be followed or altered depending on what teachers believe will work best in their classrooms.

Figure 7.1. Curriculum Map for Preparing Young Children to Be Good Digital Citizens and Prevent Cyberbullying

Gather Information at the Beginning of the School Year

- Before or at the beginning of the school year, distribute and analyze parent questionnaires to ascertain children's home experience with digital technology and social media.
- Before or at the beginning of the school year, reach out to former teachers of this year's class to ascertain if and how they addressed face-to-face and/or online teasing and bullying as well as use of digital technology and social media.

(Figure 7.1 continues on the next page)

Figure 7.1. Curriculum Map for Preparing Young Children to Be Good Digital Citizens and Prevent Cyberbullying *(continued)*

- Observe children at play in classroom or during recess to gather information about imaginary play related to digital technology as well as incidents of face-to-face teasing and bullying.

Establish Classroom Rules

- Within the first week of school, in dialogue with students, establish and post classroom rules about what it means to be a good classroom and school citizen.

Conduct Activities to Provide or Refresh Shared Language
About Face-to-Face Teasing and Bullying

- Introduce activities that provide or refresh familiarity with a shared language about face-to-face teasing and bullying.
- Introduce activities designed to prevent and address face-to-face teasing and bullying.

Conduct Classroom Discussions About Digital Technology and Social Media

- Conduct class discussion, informed by parent feedback, to ascertain children's experiences with digital technology and social media.*
- Provide activities that introduce/remind children of the names of various digital technology tools.*

Establish Classroom Rules and Provide Direct Experiences
About the Meaning of Good Digital Citizenship

- In dialogue with students, establish classroom rules about what it means to be a good digital citizen.*
- Introduce an online social media experience for children in the class.*

Conduct a Class Discussion About Online Teasing and Bullying

- Conduct an activity on the meaning of courage.*

Address the Concepts of Privacy and Permanence

- Conduct a concrete activity about understanding privacy.*
- Conduct a concrete activity about the meaning of permanent.*

Establish a Buddy System with Students in Higher Grades

- Conduct an activity to introduce students to buddies from a higher grade.*
- Conduct an ongoing online experience that promotes opportunities for students to communicate with their buddies from the higher grades.*
- Conduct a culminating activity regarding good digital citizenship.*

---

* Examples of the activities are provided in the next section of this book. The others are ones that are already undoubtedly familiar to classroom teachers or, as in the case of face-to-face teasing and bullying, can be found on many websites.

GATHERING INFORMATION
AT THE BEGINNING OF THE SCHOOL YEAR

An information gathering phase should be launched at the beginning of the school year and should coincide with setting the tone for promoting face-to-face prosocial behavior within the classroom.

Gathering Information from Parents

A first preventive measure for combating cyberbullying is to ascertain the exposure and experiences of the children in the class. In keeping with sound early childhood educational principles, K–3 teachers assess students' prior experience as a starting place when implementing new curricular topics. In tackling the topic of good digital citizenship, an important first step is to query parents about their children's home experience with digital technology and social media. (See Appendix B for a letter from a computer teacher at PS 321 to parents of older students.)

Questionnaires can be sent out before or during the first week or two of the school year or handed out in the first parent meeting. In either case, a cover letter explaining the questionnaire will serve to alert parents and other family members to the fact that teachers are planning to deal with good digital citizenship. Parents' responses will provide insight about the actual experiences students have had, and these experiences can be referenced in moving forward with this work. (See Appendix C for a sample letter and questionnaire for grades K–3.)

Although teachers are not in a position to replicate research studies about home use of technology, they can borrow and adapt information-gathering techniques that have been used by researchers to determine media exposure at home. Parent diaries are an excellent way to introduce and actively involve parents in a whole-class or whole-school approach to combating cyberbullying. An invitation to parents to document their children's media use can be followed by parent meetings in which they can share the information they have gathered. Administrators and teachers can then use these meetings as a way to launch a schoolwide anti-cyberbullying curriculum, explaining how it will unfold in the early grades and connect to efforts in the upper grades of elementary school.

Gathering Information from Other Teachers

Many elementary schools already have schoolwide policies to combat face-to-face teasing and bullying, in which case teachers will be familiar with the approach the school is taking and with curricular activities that are employed at each grade level. However, in the absence of a schoolwide policy, teachers should investigate whether and how this has been addressed by their students' former teachers.

It is important to know whether children are familiar with terminology such as teasing, bullying, and bystander, as this is the starting place for addressing cyberbullying. It is also important to know what classroom experiences 1st-, 2nd-, and 3rd-grade children had with technology or with the topic of cyberbullying in previous school years.

Observing Children at Play

In addition to gathering information from parents and former teachers, teachers should pay close attention to the content of children's play and social interactions as soon as school begins in the fall. In kindergarten classrooms where children have opportunities to engage in imaginary play, what roles do they assume? Do they try to exclude others as they engage in activities during choice time? Do they pretend to talk on cellphones or mimic texting? Who do they pretend to talk to, and what do they say? Are there opportunities for children in the early elementary grades to use tablets or computers and, if so, to what end? How do students interact as they work or play games together online within the school setting? For all children in grades K–3, are there observed incidents of face-to-face teasing and bullying within the classroom or in the schoolyard? Do there seem to be in-groups that exclude some children? These observations can be used as conversation starters about children's perceptions about teasing and bullying and use of social media.

ESTABLISH CLASSROOM RULES

Another essential measure for preventing future teasing and bullying, be it face-to-face or via social media, is to create and explicitly promote a prosocial classroom and school culture. This will serve as the foundation for a proactive stance against cyberbullying. It is important to first assess children's understanding of what it means to be a good classroom and school citizen before setting expectations and providing activities to foster good digital citizenship.

Every classroom and school has rules for behavior that are usually made explicit at the very beginning of each school year. During the first week of school, teachers typically create a set of classroom rules, and the professional literature urges that these rules be developed in collaboration with students to maximize understanding and buy-in. When rules for classroom behavior are discussed, the discussion should include what it means to be respectful of classmates and how to go about expressing one's own feelings and acknowledging the feelings of others. Within the social–emotional realm, the collaborative discussions should focus on feelings—how to use words to let others know how you feel and how to listen to and respond to others as they express their feelings.

Although establishing classroom rules is an essential precursor to establishing rules about good digital citizenship, we do not offer a specific plan for the former because we presume that all teachers establish classroom rules early in the school year. These rules, which are ideally created in dialogue with students, set the tone for promoting prosocial behavior and serve as a point of reference for later tackling rules for good digital citizenship.

CONDUCT ACTIVITIES TO PROVIDE OR REFRESH SHARED LANGUAGE ABOUT FACE-TO-FACE TEASING AND BULLYING

A good starting place for all K–3 teachers is to provide or refresh students' familiarity with a shared language about face-to-face teasing and bullying. By the time children are in kindergarten, they are likely to have direct experience with teasing and bullying, be it as victims or bystanders at home or in the neighborhood, on the school bus, in the schoolyard, and even in the classroom (Gropper & Froschl, 2000). From a developmental perspective, conversations that draw on their experience enable them to make better sense of vocabulary related to teasing and bullying that will lay important groundwork for a focus on cyberbullying.

In schools where a schoolwide anti–teasing and bullying curriculum has been adopted and is introduced at the kindergarten level, 1st-, 2nd-, and 3rd-grade teachers can draw on what was covered in kindergarten to continue the conversation about face-to-face teasing and bullying. In schools where there is no schoolwide anti–teasing and bullying curriculum, this is most certainly the starting point for kindergarten teachers who can search the Web and/or consult with the school librarian to identify curricular resources in this regard. Teachers in grades 1–3 will also want to start here unless they know for a fact that the topic was addressed across all the kindergarten classrooms.

Because the issue of face-to-face teasing and bullying is not a focus of this book, we do not offer activity plans in this regard. However, we do offer an annotated list of children's books, including some very recently published, that focus on face-to-face teasing and bullying. K–3 teachers can use such books to introduce concepts and vocabulary related to teasing and bullying. (See Part IV: Resources.)

CONDUCT CLASSROOM DISCUSSIONS ABOUT DIGITAL TECHNOLOGY AND SOCIAL MEDIA

Informed by parent feedback about their children's experience with digital technology and social media, teachers can decide on a timely juncture for leading a discussion with their students about their familiarity with various digital technologies and social media. An activity for doing so is offered in Part III: Classroom Activities. Teachers can use the activity plan that is offered as is, or they can adapt it to include additional technologies or social media mentioned by parents as ones their children use. It is wise to focus on those with which at least some children have already had experience.

After a discussion with children about their experience with digital tools, it is time to show actual tools—those that are already familiar to children as well as any that are not. For example, it is likely that all children have seen and had some experience with cellphones, but not all children have necessarily used a personal computer or tablet. This activity is designed for them to have opportunities to manipulate the tools in ways that are developmentally appropriate.

ESTABLISH CLASSROOM RULES AND PROVIDE DIRECT EXPERIENCES ABOUT THE MEANING OF GOOD DIGITAL CITIZENSHIP

Because of the emphasis on prosocial behavior in early childhood classrooms, we presume that there are many opportunities, beginning with the first day of school when teachers talk with children about how to treat classmates and the meaning of friendship. As the school year progresses, these discussions continue to arise as teachers mediate conflicts that are developmentally predictable for children who are in transition from egocentric thinking, in which they do not always perceive and respond to the needs and feelings of others when they conflict with their own.

In Part III: Classroom Activities, you will find "Creating Rules for Good Digital Citizenship," which uses a story about Cyberville, a place where there are no rules, to draw children into a discussion in which they generate rules for good digital citizenship.

Online Social Media Experience

It is within the context of promoting prosocial behavior that teachers can introduce children to an activity in which they interact with their classmates through a selected social medium, be it Google Chat or some other app, depending on children's literacy levels. If children are not yet writing and reading words, teachers should look for apps where children can post photos or perhaps communicate by drawing directly onto the app. Teachers will want to preview the writings, photos, and drawings that children want to post to ensure that they are appropriate to share with others and do not jeopardize privacy or put children at risk of uploading anything that might harm their public image.

Because a multitude of apps designed for young children are readily available and new ones are continually appearing, we recommend that teachers go to the website of the National Association for the Education of Young Children for guidelines about selecting apps that are educationally sound and appropriate for young children (naeyc.org/search/apps%20 for%20young%20children).

Again, we caution against introducing this topic in kindergarten classrooms unless it is clear that children have already been communicating with peers through social media. From a developmental perspective, if they have no prior experience in doing so it may be premature to introduce such experiences to kindergartners, who are still in the early stages of moving from egocentrism to more socially aware peer relationships.

Providing one or more online social experiences within the classroom can lead to a dialogue with children about the meaning of citizenship online. This dialogue can in turn lead to establishing a set of rules about what it means to be a good digital citizen.

Conduct a Class Discussion About Online Teasing and Bullying

Once children have had one or more online social experiences with their classmates, they can consider what teasing and bullying might look like online. In Part III, there is an activity about doing the right thing as a form of courage. Introducing or reviewing the meaning of the word "bystander" as it applies to face-to-face teasing and bullying, this activity concretizes its meaning in the world of social media and encourages children to find the courage to take an active role in combating bullying online when they witness it.

Addressing Concepts of Privacy and Permanence

As children's experience with social media expands, it is important for them to understand the concepts of privacy and permanence. Activities to address these concepts also appear in Part III. They promote understanding of privacy and permanence with concrete activities to introduce the meaning of these terms and then extend children's understanding of how these concepts apply to social media.

Adults have their own sensibilities about what they consider private information, but certainly passwords, Social Security numbers, and bank account information are among them. Children may not yet know their Social Security numbers or anything about their parents' bank accounts, but passwords are relevant as soon as they use digital media, be it their own passwords or the passwords of other family members. When teachers make use of social media as an educational tool, it is time to teach children about passwords and password protection.

Privacy relates to communications that children have on social media, particularly if these exchanges occur outside of school. By 1st grade, some children may text or chat with friends online and may already have a Facebook page. Although these kinds of exchanges occur outside of school, teachers have an important role to play in making children aware that what they post may end up being seen by unintended viewers and that whatever they choose to post should be in the spirit of what it means to be a good digital citizen.

Furthermore, children should be introduced early on in their use of social media to the meaning of the word "permanence" in the digital world. Once photos or written information is posted and shared in the digital world, it doesn't disappear. Emails can be forwarded to others, texts can be shown to others, and Facebook can be seen by unknown viewers. Helping children see social media as a social forum in which we want to be our best selves is as important as emphasizing the respect for privacy in regard to communications received by friends who may not want their communications shared.

Establishing a Buddy System with Students in Higher Grades

It is a common practice in many schools to enlist students in higher grades to work one-on-one on literacy or other activities with children in the primary grades. These buddy systems are seen as advantageous to both the younger and the older child. It is also an excellent strategy for promoting good digital citizenship among students at different grade levels and is particularly salient in schools that take a whole-school approach to addressing cyberbullying.

The older students undoubtedly will be more fully immersed in social media and can serve as models of prosocial behavior in that world. Teachers at the early childhood level can initiate a buddy system with their colleagues at higher grade levels and from there organize a series of activities so that buddies can meet each other face to face and have multiple opportunities to exhibit good digital citizenship as they communicate with each other through the appropriate social medium that exists within the school.

Finally, buddies can collaborate in a culminating activity in which they document what it means to be a good digital citizen. This can include not only how to interact with others in positive, prosocial ways but also how, as bystanders, to confront cyberbullying in a way that protects any peer who is the recipient. Such buddy-to-buddy work can be initially done in pairs, but eventually the entire participating early childhood and upper-grade classes can collaborate on a culminating activity that serves as a statement of the meaning of good digital citizenship that can be promulgated to the larger school community. Suggestions for building good digital citizenship through upper- and lower-grade partnerships can be found in Part III.

CLASSROOM ACTIVITIES

INTRODUCTION TO ACTIVITIES

There are many opportunities to integrate learning about good digital citizenship into the daily life of the classroom. The activities in this section are within the scope of traditional K–3 curricula addressing social–emotional learning, executive function, literacy development, and conceptual development.

Social–emotional learning (SEL) has always been the core of early elementary education and is now increasingly understood to be a critical factor from kindergarten through high school. Once thought of as "soft skills," studies show that children who attend programs that focus on social–emotional learning do better academically, have higher rates of attendance, and are safer in school (Epstein, 2009). The Collaborative for Academic, Social, and Emotional Learning (CASEL) defines these skills as self-awareness, self-management, social awareness, responsible decisionmaking, and relationship skills.

Executive function, a term that has emerged from brain research, is defined as a wide range of central control processes in the brain that link and categorize cognitive, motor, and behavioral responses that enable goal setting, planning, and accomplishing tasks. Development of these processes begins in early childhood and continues to grow until people reach their early 20s (Gartrell, 2013). As is the case with SEL, early attention to executive function skill development improves children's ability to focus, make decisions, and get along with their peers.

Literacy, the ability to read, write, and use oral language as a means of communication, is developed in a classroom that is rich in print—picture books, chapter books, charts, and vocabulary-building word webs that are displayed around the classroom. It is further strengthened by spoken stories, followed by opportunities for children to discuss their reactions and ideas. In the digital age, creating a literate community also includes audio books, online activities, and literacy lessons taught on tablets and whiteboards.

Conceptual development refers to the intellectual growth that is fostered by a literacy-centered learning environment. Through stories and discussion, thinking becomes more logical and rational. Rules and "doing the right thing" become important, and the ability to show concern and see another's point of view are developed. Reading and early writing (or dictation) provide a means to articulate ideas and emotions. Gains in oral communication and listening skills help children resolve conflicts peacefully, using language instead of physical aggression. Cooperation, supported by classroom rules regarding inclusion, help children to work and play in groups, whether online or in the classroom.

The familiar teaching strategies that form the basis for the activities that follow incorporate the core principles of early childhood teaching and learning outlined previously. Literacy is the framework for activities that embed SEL, executive function, and conceptual development. Through charting, story and discussion, word webs, vignettes, puppet plays, writing, and interacting with older students, children are building their "literate community," in preparation for becoming good digital citizens. Suggestions are included for conducting activities online for classrooms where whiteboards, tablets, or computers are in use. Activities with multiple parts can be used over time and as issues come up. The word webs and charts are meant to grow as the school year progresses, and more vocabulary related to good digital citizenship is needed. Children should be invited to suggest books or online games that support good digital citizenship.

In each classroom, it is the teacher who is the best judge of how and when to use the activities. Some schools may have a whole-school approach to digital citizenship already in place, whereas others may depend on the interest and knowledge of individual teachers. The range of technology use is wide; in some schools kindergartners use tablets, and in other schools the use of technology may not start until grades 4–5. For most kindergarten children, it is more likely that the emphasis will be on addressing face-to-face bullying rather than cyberbullying. Fortunately, there is a rich body of children's literature on this issue that goes back to the beginnings of early childhood education. The annotated bibliography includes selections from classics and more contemporary picture books.

However, since the research has clearly established that children at ever younger ages are online, it is imperative that teaching and learning about good digital citizenship become part of early childhood education for reasons of safe and responsible use at any age and as a prevention for cyberbullying.

Note: These activities are adapted with permission from Right from the Start, a national FHI 360 initiative designed to lay the groundwork for children in grades pre-K–3 to be safe and responsible digital citizens. For more information about FHI 360, visit fhi360.org/projects/right-start-digital-age-fhi-360-national-initiative.

ACTIVITY #1: DISCOVERING WHAT WE KNOW

Skills: Literacy, conceptual development

Materials: Photos of computer, mobile or smartphone, tablet, laptop, earbuds (be sure the pictures are large enough to be visible for everyone); chart paper on easel, markers

Time: 15–20 minutes (multiple sessions as needed)

It is a given that children will arrive at school with some knowledge of the digital world. It may be that they have seen family members using cellphones. There may be a computer located in a central part of their home. Some children may have had Skype or FaceTime visits with grandparents or other relatives. Others may have used digital devices at home with a parent or older sibling nearby. However, there also may be children in your class that have had no experience at all with digital devices.

So, an important first step for children entering the digital world within the classroom is to determine their range of knowledge about digital devices. Class meeting is a good time to have a discussion. Here are some suggestions for getting started.

Activity

Gather photos of commonly used digital devices, such as mobile or smartphones, tablets, laptops, or desktop computers. Mount the photos on chart paper so that there is room to record the conversation underneath each device.

Display the photo of one object at a time on an easel. Be sure everyone can see it clearly.

In a class meeting, introduce the activity.

Teacher: "Today, we have some interesting pictures to talk about. Please remember to raise your hand when you want to speak. We want to hear from everyone."

Ask children a series of questions about the object:

- Has anyone ever seen this object?
- Can you tell us something that you know about it?
- Does anyone know what it is called?
- Does someone in your family use this device?
- Have you ever used it?

Write down under the photo what the children have said. If they have named the object accurately, write the name at the top of the list. If not, tell children the accurate name.

Explain that these devices are what we use when we want to talk or play or connect with someone on a screen instead of in person. This is what is called being "online."

Continue to mount and discuss photos. The discussion can take place over several days.

Each time, repeat the definition of being "online."

Display the charts in one section of the room—if possible, near the classroom computer or media center.

Follow-Up Activity: More Digital Discoveries

Skills: Conceptual development

Materials: Digital device picture charts previously developed; tablet, mobile, or smartphone; interactive whiteboard

Time: 20 minutes

In a class meeting, briefly review the digital devices picture charts.

Ask children to say the name of each device and tell what they know about it. (Remind children to raise their hands before speaking and encourage full sentences.)

Say, "Today I have an actual _____ [name the device you are showing, for example, a tablet] to show you. Everyone will have a turn to look it over. The tablet needs to be handled carefully, so after your turn, please pass it carefully to your neighbor."

After each child has explored the device, talk about its uses. If children will be using the device in class, talk about when and how it will be used. "We will be using the tablet when we go online."

If the classroom has an interactive whiteboard, introduce it and demonstrate how it works by showing an interactive program that will be fun and exciting for the class. Choose an app or program that is safe and fun and that demonstrates good digital citizenship.

Note: At a parent meeting or through an online survey, you already may have received parent feedback about children's experiences with digital technology and social media. See Appendix C for a sample parent letter and questionnaire.

ACTIVITY #2: CREATING RULES FOR GOOD DIGITAL CITIZENSHIP

Skills: Literacy, conceptual development

Materials: Chart paper, markers, tape for mounting chart

Time: 15–20 minutes

Once you have established rules for the classroom and for outdoor spaces and you have assessed the children's familiarity with digital media devices, it is a good idea to extend the "rules" to online activities. The story below, "Cyberville: A Place with No Rules," provides a fun way to start the process. It provides the opportunity to discuss why rules for online activities are needed, and it is a catalyst for developing online rules in the classroom and at home. A few discussion starters follow the story, but it is important to let children create their own rules with adult facilitation. The rules can be written on chart paper and displayed near the classroom media center. It is a good idea to revisit the rules periodically and add to them as other ideas come up.

Note: If you have conducted the introductory activity, "Discovering What We Know," remind children that using digital devices like smartphones and tablets are the way we go online.

Activity

During a class meeting, introduce the story: "Today, I have a story to tell you. It's not in a book, and it has no pictures, but it will make you think. Listen very carefully so we can talk about the story later."

Cyberville: A Place with No Rules

Once upon a right now time there was a place named Cyberville. Cyberville was in outer space. It was in the cloud. Grown-ups and children didn't actually live in Cyberville. They lived in big cities and small towns and on farms or ranches. Everyone traveled to Cyberville on their tablets, their smartphones, or their computers. Traveling to Cyberville was called "going online."

Cyberville was a fun and exciting place. You could go there to play games with friends. You could go there to learn about new places and people, and you could write messages to your friends and even connect with children in faraway places. You could go there to find out about things that interest you, like art or baseball, or motors or animals. In fact, you could find out about almost anything in Cyberville.

But Cyberville had a problem, and it was a big one. THERE WERE NO RULES! Children had rules at home to keep them safe and clean and healthy.

In school, there were rules about taking turns and sharing toys, treating one another kindly and respectfully, and safety rules like "Walk, don't run, in the halls."

Grown-ups, too, had rules at work and at home. People had to treat one another with respect at work, and families had many rules for safe and kind behavior. Even cities and towns had rules. There were rules for crossing streets, driving at safe speeds, and not littering. All the rules were made by people to make life orderly and pleasant for everyone.

What happened in Cyberville? It just grew up so fast it got to be a place with no rules. That wasn't so good. Sometimes strangers tried to sell things to children. Sometimes grown-ups sent mean messages to other grown-ups. Sometimes a child got angry at a friend and said something online to hurt that friend's feelings. Sometimes children who were playing a game in Cyberville wouldn't let other children join in, which led to bad feelings all around. Doing and saying mean things in Cyberville led to another big problem. If you said something mean, you couldn't take it back! Mean messages in Cyberville couldn't be erased and lots of people could see them, even if you didn't want them to.

After reading the story, have a brief discussion about if and how children are going online. Here are some discussion starters:

- Do you go online?
- If so, what is your favorite thing to do online?
- What is your favorite device? A phone? A laptop? A tablet?
- Does your family have some online rules? What are they?
- Do you know anyone who has been sent a hurtful online message?
- Do you know anyone who had a stranger try to sell them things online?

When it's clear that children understand the concept of being online, ask, "Why is Cyberville having these problems? What would you do to solve Cyberville's problems?" Write down all their ideas.

Children may come up with the idea of creating rules for Cyberville on their own. If not, you can suggest that making a few rules for Cyberville could make it an even better place. Ask, "What are your ideas for Cyberville rules?" Suggest: "Let's create a chart of rules for Cyberville. I will write down your ideas, and we can put the chart in the media center (or near the computer) to remind us about good and responsible online behavior."

As children come up with ideas, guide them into forming full sentences for placing their ideas on the chart. Explain that the rules for Cyberville are rules for "good online citizenship" and should be used for being online in the classroom, at home, and in the world.

Mount the chart near the classroom media center.

Revisit the rules from time to time and update them as necessary.

Online Version of the "Rules" Chart

If you are already using technology in your classroom, the "Rules" chart can be uploaded to the classroom computer(s) or electronic whiteboard and reviewed at the beginning of each activity. If students have tablets for classroom work, the "Rules" can become a screen saver that appears before the work begins.

Follow-Up Activity: Using Our Rules Online

Skills: Literacy, conceptual development

Materials: Tablets

Time: 15–20 minutes

Set up a Google Chat, Hangout, or other online communication platform that is used in your school. You will need to facilitate the activity to ensure that children's posts are safe and appropriate for sharing.

Explain that there will be an online chat in which everyone can participate. Set the topic; it could be about

- favorite places to go, actually or by imagination
- favorite animals and why you like them
- favorite TV shows and/or movies

Notes:

Be careful not to have topics that involve family privacy.

Before the "chat" begins, review the online rules that the children developed for "Cyberville."

If children are not yet ready to write to one another, select an app that uses pictures instead of words.

ACTIVITY #3: WORD WEBS AND CHARTS: BUILDING VOCABULARY FOR DIGITAL CITIZENSHIP

Skills: Literacy, social–emotional, conceptual development

Materials: Whiteboard, chart paper, markers

Time: 15–20 minutes per session

Participation in the digital world opens up a wide range of new vocabulary learning for children. In the process of acquiring language, children may use words they hear frequently without necessarily understanding what the words mean. Creating colorful word webs and charts to display near the classroom computer, in the computer lab, or on a whiteboard will help children increase their vocabulary and grasp of words about good digital citizenship, technology, and online safety.

Building vocabulary is an ongoing activity. The webs and charts can expand as children experience more online activities. They also can be uploaded to the classroom whiteboard and be brought up for review and additions before and after relevant lessons.

Activity: Part One—Learning Important Online Words

Bring children together for a meeting.

Introduce the activity according to the way children will be going online, such as working on tablets, on classroom computers, in a computer lab, and/or on a whiteboard. Say, "Now that our class is going to do some of our work online, we need to learn some important words for those activities. Let's create a chart of vocabulary words about being online."

Ask children for suggestions about what to call the chart—for example, "Our Online Words" or "Our Web-Words."

Say, "Does anyone know some words about being online?" Note children's responses on the chart.

Guide the discussion so that key words and definitions are listed on the chart. Here is an example:

Our Online Words

Password: A private code word we choose that lets you get online.

NOTE: In many schools, one password is used by everyone. If this applies to your school, say, "In our school, the password is XXX."

Internet: A network that connects computers around the world.

Log off: To leave a program or leave the Internet.

Log on: To sign on to an Internet site using a password.

Cellphone: A phone that you can take with you and use anywhere you go.

NOTE: You might want to make the distinction between a smartphone, which is connected to the Internet, and a flip phone, which is not.

Download: The way to bring information into your computer from an Internet site.

Digital: A coding system using the numbers 1 and 0 that is the language for computers.

Digital media: Video, audio, and software programs that are created and stored through digital coding using the numbers 1 and 0.

Hashtag: A # symbol that comes before a short online message like a tweet.

App: A shortened form of "application," which is a small program you can easily download.

Blog: A place to share ideas with other people on a special website.

Post the chart in an area of the classroom where online activities will take place. If you have a whiteboard, upload the chart for periodic review.

It is a good idea to start the word web with a few words—such as Internet, log on, log off, cellphone, and download—and add vocabulary as computer use increases during the school year.

Activity: Part Two—Digital Citizenship Chart

In a class meeting, introduce the idea of a new word web.

Say, "Now that you play games and we do some of our work online, let's create a chart to remind us about how to treat one another online. For the classroom we say, Good Community Members. For playing and working online, let's say Good Digital Citizenship."

Guide children as they produce a chart about Good Digital Citizenship. Be sure the chart includes phrases such as the following:

- We treat each other kindly online.
- We include everyone in online games.
- We respect each other online.

As children gain more experience with being online, revisit the chart often and add phrases about empathy, courage, and privacy; for example,

- We stand by our friends, in our classroom and online.
- We never write mean messages online.
- We know that mean online messages hurt—and they are permanent, which means they never go away.

- We never share private information about ourselves, our family, or our friends online.

Activity: Part Three—Online Safety Word Web

As children become more adept and independent in using the Internet, they need to be made aware of dangers related to being online. A word web about caution should be posted in the digital media center or near the place where children work or play online. The safety issue needs to be balanced with the benefits that come with access to the information, fun, and learning the Internet provides.

In a class meeting, tell children that when they are online in school or at home, they need to learn how to be safe. Compare safety online to safety in the everyday world.

To begin, go over well-known safety rules about crossing streets, not talking to strangers, and always knowing how to find a trusted adult when you need help.

Say, "Just like we know how to be safe in the real world, we need to keep ourselves safe when we are online."

Let's make a chart to remind us about Online Safety.

Guide the discussion so that key issues emerge:

- Never talk to strangers online.
- If a new screen pops up while you are online, show an adult right away.
- If someone posts a mean remark about you, ask a trusted adult for help immediately.
- Never post personal or private information online.
- Never tell anyone except a trusted adult your password.

For a glossary of key Internet vocabulary, see Appendix D.

ACTIVITY #4: DOING THE RIGHT THING: A FORM OF COURAGE

Skills: Literacy, social–emotional, executive function, conceptual development

Materials: Chart paper and markers, *Nobody Knew What to Do*, by Becky Ray McCain*

Time: 15–20 minutes for Part One; 20–30 minutes for Part Two

Through a powerful story, discussion, and follow-up activities, children "listen to their strong side" and learn how not to be a bystander to face-to-face or cyberbullying. The activities look at courage, not as feats of daring heroics as seen on TV and in online games, but as "doing the right thing." Examples of courage include standing up for a friend, not being a bystander, and not succumbing to peer pressure. A preliminary activity ensures that children understand two key vocabulary words: bystander and courage.

Activity: Part One

In a class meeting, tell children that you have a terrific story to read to them during story time, but first they need to think about some new vocabulary words.

Write the word "bystander" on the chart and ask children to raise their hands if they have an idea of what it means. Note their ideas on the chart.

To spur their thinking, prompt children to see that there are two words combined. If needed, remind children about previous discussions about bullying.

Guide the discussion to a definition of bystander:

A person who sees something harmful happening but doesn't do anything.

Next, write the word "courage" on the chart.

As above, ask children for their ideas about what the word "courage" means.

If anyone mentions the word "brave," use it to guide a discussion about doing the right thing.

Give an example of courage as doing the right thing:

When Tammy noticed that kids were mimicking Joy because she sometimes used Chinese words instead of English, she told them to "quit it." She befriended Joy and made sure the other kids didn't tease her again.

Ask children to keep the words "bystander" and "courage" in their minds for the upcoming story and for doing the right thing every day.

Activity: Part Two

Nobody Knew What to Do is a story about how one child found the courage to do the right thing and tell the teacher about Ray, who was being picked on by a class bully. Together with the teacher and other children who did not want to be bystanders, Ray was befriended and the bully was defeated. The story about face-to-face bullying is an excellent segue into talking about cyberbullying.

Read the story to children and lead a discussion using some questions to facilitate their thinking:

- Do you think the main character (name the person) did the right thing to speak to his teacher?
- Why do you think so?
- Was he a bystander? Were the other children bystanders? What made them bystanders? (If needed, refer back to the definition on the chart.)
- Talk about the elements in the story that demonstrate courage.
- Did it take courage to tell the teacher?
- Ask, "Can anyone think of a situation where someone stood up for themselves or for a friend that was having a problem?"
- Why would it be courageous to not be a bystander? For example, to stop someone from saying mean things about someone online?

Nobody Knew What to Do by Becky Ray McCain is available through libraries, local bookstores, Amazon, Barnes & Noble and is available for listening on YouTube (youtu.be/plB6Vp0uHK8).

Follow-Up Activity: Stopping a Cyberbully

Skills: Social–emotional, conceptual development

Materials: Storyboard or story displayed on a whiteboard

Time: 20 minutes

At a class meeting, introduce the story: "Today, I have a story about the courage to not be a bystander. It's not in a book and it has no pictures, so you will need to listen very carefully. It may help you concentrate to close your eyes while I'm telling it, but promise you won't go to sleep! Remember, a cyberbully is someone who says hurtful things or threatens someone online. Here's the story."

How Class 501 Stopped a Cyberbully

Fifth-graders in class 501 at Wesley School had a big problem. There was a cyberbully writing awful text and email messages about one boy in the class. Everyone in the class knew about it because they all saw the messages. Some girls and boys were embarrassed to read the messages; it made them feel sad to see someone being hurt. But some others laughed at the messages and taunted the boy in class.

One day the boy who was being cyberbullied didn't come to school. He didn't come the next day and the day after that either. The children began to wonder why he wasn't there. Finally, after a whole week went by, the teacher called a meeting to tell the children that the boy who was being cyberbullied did not want to come to their school anymore and was going to transfer to a different school.

This made the children who didn't like the cyberbullying feel worse than ever. They didn't want the boy to transfer, and they were sorry to have been bystanders. They decided to take action!

First, they wrote text and email messages to the boy apologizing for the mean behavior. Then, a few students and the teacher talked privately to the boy who had written the mean messages, and he apologized, too. After their experience with cyberbullying, class 501 started a 5th-grade campaign to stop cyberbullying. Students got other 5th-grade classes in the school to join in. Soon, there were STOP CYBERBULLYING posters in all the school hallways.

The boy did return to school, and his classmates made him feel very welcome. He joined the Stop Cyberbullying campaign. The person who had sent the mean messages never was a cyberbully again.

Start the discussion by asking some questions:

- How did the story make you feel?
- Were the other children bystanders?
- Why do you think some of the children in the story felt sad?
- Did you think the children who started the Stop Cyberbullying campaign were courageous? Why?
- Did class 501 "do the right thing"?

Follow-Up Activity: "Do the Right Thing" Puppet Play

Skills: Social–emotional, literacy, conceptual development

Materials: Three popsicle sticks, paper bags, or other classroom puppets to represent three children

Time: 15–20 minutes

Note: You will need to play all three parts for this activity.

At class meeting or story time, tell the children, "These puppets are having a problem and they need your help."
    Play out the scenario for the children.

> *Puppet 1:* I'm so mad at Carrie.
> *Puppet 2:* Why?
> *Puppet 1:* She really, really hurt my feelings when she said my hair is ugly.
> *Puppet 2:* That was mean. What are you going to do?
> *Puppet 1:* I'm going to say something mean back—and I'm going to do it online so everyone can see it!
> *Puppet 2:* Wow! That will get back at her.
> *Puppet 3:* Hi, what are you doing?
> *Puppet 1:* We're planning to send Carrie a message online.
> *Puppet 3:* Can I do it with you?
> *Puppets 1 and 2:* Sure.
> *Puppet 1:* I'm going to write, "Carrie has ugly clothes."
> *Puppet 3:* Hey, wait a minute. Our rules say, don't be mean online.
> *Puppet 1:* I know. But she was mean to me.
> *Puppet 3:* Was it online?
> *Puppet 1:* No, but . . .
> The three puppets are sitting at a table with a tablet in front of them.

End the scenario here and ask:

- Can you help the puppets solve their problem?
- Did Puppet 1 have a reason to feel angry and hurt?
- Would putting a mean message online be doing the right thing?
- What did Puppet 3 say? Was that the right thing?
- Do you think the puppets should talk to Carrie about what she said?
- Do you think they need to ask a teacher for help?

After children have had practice doing puppet plays with scenarios you have created, ask if anyone has an idea for another scenario about being online. Help the children shape their ideas into a puppet play. If they elect to use puppets, they can select some that are in the classroom or they can make their own simple stick puppets. Help children select players and practice their scenario before presenting it to the class.

ACTIVITY #5: WHAT DOES PERMANENT MEAN?
A WORD EXPERIMENT

Skills: Executive function, conceptual development, literacy

Materials: Chart paper, plastic sheet protectors, washable and permanent markers, small sponges or damp paper towels. With a permanent marker, draw a line down the center of each plastic sheet and mark one side W and the other side P.

Time: 20 minutes, plus ongoing daily checkups

Permanence is an abstract concept that would not have been taught about in early primary classrooms prior to the digital age. The idea that something we post online is not erasable is difficult for adults and children alike to comprehend. Therefore, permanence is a concept we must help children understand. The activity and vignette that follow address the concept of permanence in developmentally appropriate ways.

Activity

In a class meeting:

Explain that everyone is going to conduct a word experiment. The word is "permanent."

Ask, "Does anyone have an idea about what that word means?" Acknowledge any ideas.

Help children arrive at a definition; for example, permanent means long-lasting or everlasting, which means it cannot be taken away.

Ask children, "Did you know that when we write words online, they become permanent?" Explain, "Once they are written, they cannot be taken away."

Say, "Let's do an experiment to help us understand more about what the word 'permanent' means."

Ask children to sit at their tables or desks to do the experiment.

Distribute the plastic sheet protectors and put separate containers of washable/permanent markers on each table. Label the containers and ask children to be careful not to mix them up.

Note: If children sit at desks, give each child a plastic sheet and two markers. Mark the permanent marker with a piece of masking tape to avoid any mix-up.

Ask each child to print her or his name on each side of the sheet. Then, children can continue to write their names or make little drawings down the rest of the sheet, using a washable marker on the "W" side and permanent marker on the "P" side.

Distribute small pieces of damp sponges or damp paper towels.

Ask children to apply the sponge to the "W" side of the sheet. Talk about what happens.

Do the same to the "P" side of the sheet. Talk about what happens.

Reiterate the definition of the word "permanent" and remind children to think about the experiment when they are online.

Post the definition of permanent near the class computer or digital media center of the room. Remind children of the experiment over time to keep them aware of the fact that what they post becomes permanent.

Follow-Up Activity: A Problem-Solving Vignette and Discussion

Skills: Executive function, conceptual development, literacy

Materials: Vignette printed on chart paper or projected on whiteboard

Time: 20 minutes

Haley and Jamila were best friends in 2nd grade. They worked together, ate lunch together, and always joined the same jump rope game at recess. Haley was absent from school for a whole week because she had the flu. While she was out, Jamila became good friends with Jessie. When Haley came back to school, Jamila wanted to include Jessie in all the things she used to do with Haley. This made Haley feel angry and jealous.

Haley thought about writing something mean about Jessie online so Jamila wouldn't like her anymore. But Haley knew that an online message would be permanent and that everyone in class would see it. The class had done an experiment about the word "permanent" in class, and there also were rules about being kind and responsible online.

But Haley still felt angry and jealous. Can you help her?

What are some ways that Haley could help herself feel better?

Should she talk about her feelings with her teacher? Her mom? Jamila?

ACTIVITY #6: UNDERSTANDING PRIVACY:
AN IMPORTANT CONCEPT FOR ONLINE ACTIVITIES

Skills: Concept development, social–emotional, executive function, literacy

Materials: Notepaper and envelopes, chart paper and markers (or tablets), vignette, pencils and paper for writing

Time: 20 minutes

Privacy is a critical concept that children engaged in online activities need to understand. It is important both for safety reasons and because revealing private matters can be emotionally harmful and have long-term consequences for children who expose private matters and for those who have confidences breached.

Activity

Prepare a brief note for each child and place it in a sealed envelope. If children are prereaders, use pictures instead of words. The note can say something simple like, "Do you have a pet?" or "I know the date of your birthday."

Introduce the activity in a class meeting:

"Good morning. Now that we chat with each other online in school and sometimes out of school, we need to learn the meaning of a very important word. I'm not going to tell you the word, but maybe, if you think hard, you will guess it after we do this activity."

Pass the notes around and say, "This envelope is just for you. You may open it, but please do not share it with anyone else. It's just for you."

After children have opened their notes, ask:

"Can anyone guess why we did this activity?"

You may need to prompt by reminding children, "Remember, I said the message was just for you."

If anyone comes up with the word "private" or "privacy," acknowledge that that is what the activity is about.

If not, supply the word. "I gave each of you a 'private' message."

Ask, "Does anyone have an idea about the meaning of the word 'private' or 'privacy'?"

Note children's ideas on the chart.

Using children's ideas as much as possible, shape working definitions of "private" and "privacy" and write them on the chart:

"Private" means information that belongs to you, your family, and
trusted adults, but not to anyone else.

"Privacy" means that personal information should be shared only with
your family or trusted adults but is not for everyone.

Explain the reason for the activity:

The activity we just did was to help us learn the importance of privacy,
especially now that we go online to do some of our schoolwork and
to communicate with our friends. To keep information private, you
should not give anyone personal information about yourself, your
family, or your friends. Online is not a place to share secrets, and
privacy is important for being safe online. Remember, when you put
something online, lots of people you may not even know can see it.

Follow-Up Activity: Creating Privacy Stories

Skills: Concept development, social–emotional, executive function, literacy

Materials: Vignette printed on chart paper or projected on a whiteboard,
tablets or pencils and paper

Time: 20 minutes

Tell children that you have a "privacy" story to share.
Read the story aloud:

Ziggy's mom was planning a big surprise party for his sister's birthday.
Grandparents and cousins were coming from far away. Ziggy was
so excited that he wanted to tell somebody the secret. He texted his
friend Jake. But Jake's sister saw the message, and she texted her good
friend, who texted another friend. Finally, someone texted Ziggy's
sister by mistake, and the surprise was spoiled.

Have a discussion about why the surprise party information was private. Remind children about the definitions of "private" and "privacy."

Ask everyone to write a short story about online privacy. They can use
the anecdote above as an example. If children are using tablets, they can
write on them. If not, use pencils and paper.

Prereading children can dictate a story.

Follow-Up Activity: Safe and Private Passwords

Skills: Concept development, social–emotional, executive function, literacy

Materials: Tablets or pencils and paper

Time: 20 minutes

In a class meeting shortly after completing the Understanding Privacy activity, ask children to review what they remember about the discussion of the words "private" and "privacy."

Read the definitions of "private" and "privacy" aloud.

Say, "Today we are going to talk about another important thing that needs to be kept private. Here's a clue: It's something we need if we want to do lessons or chat and play games with friends online. Any ideas?"

Acknowledge children's ideas and high-five if anyone comes up with "password."

Ask children why they think their password needs to be private and not shared with anyone.

Review online safety and privacy rules.

Talk about how to make a safe and private password. Ask,

- Is my street address a safe password? Why? Why not?
- Is my name and birthday a safe password? Why? Why not?
- Is my pet's name and age a safe password? Why? Why not?

Lead children to the idea that a safe password should be:

Something *only* you understand and can easily remember. For example:
- A favorite big word and number that is not your house or age, for example, Megatron20
- A favorite character from a book and a number you like, for example, Mowgli19

Have children practice writing types of passwords that would be safe, private, and easy to remember.

In closing, remind children that the passwords they created were for practice and that their real password is known only to them and a trusted adult.

ACTIVITY #7: BUILDING GOOD DIGITAL CITIZENSHIP

Skills: Executive function, social–emotional, conceptual development, literacy (for both lower- and upper-grade students)

Materials: Large construction paper or poster board, markers, pencil/paper, stick-on nametags, online communication devices (computers, interactive whiteboard, tablets)

Time: Ongoing sessions of 20–30 minutes each

Pairing children in grades K–3 with upper-grade students can be a valuable teaching and learning experience for all. Older students provide expertise in technology and experience to their "buddies" in the lower grades while gaining insight about how they were themselves a few years ago. Younger students enjoy having the attention and learning from a "big kid."

Preparation

To prepare for partnerships, propose the idea to the principal and your peers in the upper grades. Partnering grades will depend on the configuration of your school. In a K–5 school, upper grades would probably be 4–5. If you are in a school that goes through grade 8, you could partner with middle school students in grades 6, 7, or 8.

After the administrators have given approval, work with your fellow teachers to select partnering students. Together, you will need to decide how many students to recruit. If the school you are partnering with already has a policy for addressing cyberbullying, it may be that an entire upper grade will participate. However, if only one or a few classes are participating, selection criteria may include classes in which the teachers are interested in explicit discussions about fairness and good digital citizenship and in promoting an interest in partnering with younger children among their students.

Ask your upper-grade teacher partner to meet with older students and explain the purpose of the partnership. The following are some ideas to put forth:

- You will be acting as role models of good digital citizenship for the younger children.
- You can demonstrate all the ways we have discussed to prevent cyberbullying in our school.
- Children look up to older students and are happy to learn from you.
- Your knowledge of the Internet and good digital citizenship is important.
- Your job is to guide activities, not to do all the work.
- Be patient with mistakes and don't expect perfection.

Activity: Part One—Getting Started

Call a class meeting to introduce the partnership. The following are some ideas to put forth:

- Students from grade X are going to become partners with us.
- We will work in pairs (or small groups).
- They will come into our classroom to help us learn ways to be good digital citizens.
- They will become our "buddies." We'll be able to talk to them online.
- We'll do online projects together.
- It will be fun.

Activity: Part Two—Getting to Know One Another

Set up a Google Hangout (or a chat through another platform used in your school) with your students and their upper-grade partners.

Have students and upper-grade partners introduce themselves to one another and talk about familiar topics, such as pets, favorite sport or activity, favorite online games, TV shows, or movies.

As an alternative, you can set up an in-person Getting to Know One Another meeting.

Have your class write a "Welcome" letter to the older students. It can be sent by computer or hand-delivered, depending on whether digital devices are in use in your classroom.

When the older students arrive in the classroom, ask everyone to make stick-on nametags.

If you have a "welcoming song," children can sing it to their "partners."

Ask each partner group to spend a few minutes learning about one another. Suggested topics are families, pets, favorite activities, sports, and online games.

Have paper and pencils available so that students can write. Older students can write for children who still need to dictate.

My Partner and Me

Child's Name	Partner's Name
My family	My family
My pet	My pet
My favorite activity	My favorite activity
Sports I like	Sports I like
Favorite online game	Favorite online game

Have "partners" shake hands as they say goodbye to each other.

ACTIVITY #8: WORKING WITH PARTNERS

Skills: Literacy, executive function, conceptual development

Materials: Whiteboard or chart paper

Time: 20–30 minutes

Conduct a class meeting with upper-grade partners.

In advance, ask the upper-grade partners to each prepare one or two ideas about what the phrase "good digital citizenship" means to them. Ask them to also give an example of the rules they use for talking to their friends online—for example, no put-downs or teasing. Older students' ideas can be posted in large type on the whiteboard.

Before the older students arrive, tell the children about the topic for the class meeting. For example:

> Good morning everyone. Now that we are learning about how to do some activities online, our partners are coming to talk about ways to be a good digital citizen. Please listen respectfully to each person, and then you can ask questions and share some of your own ideas.

Welcome the older students to the classroom.

Have everyone introduce themselves. Note: If your first meeting was in-person, have everyone do quick re-introductions.

Have the upper-grade partners make their "Good Digital Citizenship" presentations.

Invite questions and other ideas from the children.

Have the children compose and send a "thank-you" text to the older students.

Follow-Up Activity: Stop Cyberbullying Posters

Skills: Literacy, executive function, conceptual development

Materials: Pencils, crayons, paper, poster board, markers, mounting tape

Time: Two to three 20–30-minute sessions

As a follow-up to the older student's presentation, have the partners make Good Digital Citizenship posters to display around the school.

Plan the activity to take place over two to three sessions.

Select pairs (or small groups) to work together.

Distribute paper and pencils or crayons and ask partners first to plan their posters on paper.

Provide poster board and markers for the project.

Have the partners display their posters around the school. Facilitate mounting the posters.

Have the children and their upper-grade partners report about their project in an assembly and on the school website.

Follow-Up Activity: Stop Cyberbullying PowerPoint

Skills: Literacy, executive function, conceptual development

Materials: Digital device, PowerPoint template

Time: Two to three 20–30-minute sessions

After the children in your class have done activities related to good digital citizenship and are familiar with the concept, invite the older students in to work with them on planning and producing a PowerPoint presentation.

Plan the activity to take place over two to three sessions of about 30 minutes each.

Schedule a class meeting with children and their upper-grade partners to generate ideas for the PowerPoint presentation.

Display some of the previous work about good digital citizenship—for example, definitions of permanence and privacy, and rules for password safety.

After the discussion, vote together on key points of good digital citizenship to include in the PowerPoint presentation.

Assign pairs (or small groups) to each create one to two slides.

Edit the slides as needed.

Ask the partners to generate ideas about how to share the PowerPoint digitally—for example, through the school website or at a whole-school assembly.

Disseminate the PowerPoint presentation according to their ideas.

Follow-Up Activity: Partner Project Closure

Skills: Social–emotional, literacy, executive function

Materials: Digital device, snacks, drinks

Time: 30 minutes

Have children compose and send an Evite for an end-of-project celebration to their upper-grade partners.

When the partners arrive, review all the ways the children and their upper-grade partners have worked together to promote good digital citizenship—for example, presentations, posters, or PowerPoint.

Share snacks together.

Have each child write a thank-you text to the child's upper-grade partner, including at least one idea learned about being a good digital citizen. Or have the class write a thank-you text to each partner, again listing ideas learned from them about good digital citizenship.

Part IV

RESOURCES

Picture Books About Face-to-Face Teasing and Bullying

Face-to-face teasing and bullying unfortunately has a long history in schools, the home, and the community. Consequently, a large body of children's literature, classic literature, and beloved picture books devoted to this issue is available. Titles include:

- *Chrysanthemum*, by Kevin Henkes (1991)
- *The Story of Ferdinand*, by Munro Leaf (1933)
- *Frederick* (1967) and *Swimmy* (1963), by Leo Lionni
- *Crow Boy*, by Taro Yashima (1976)
- *The Hating Book*, by Charlotte Zolotow (1989)

We urge teachers, especially kindergarten teachers, to revisit these books and other classics as a base for preparing children to become good digital citizens and prevent cyberbullying when they go online. The following annotated list contains contemporary books about face-to-face teasing and bullying:

Doering, A. F., & Shin, S. (2016). *Sometimes jokes aren't funny: What to do about hidden bullying*. North Mankato, MN: Picture Window Books (a Capstone Imprint). ISBN# 978-1-4795-6943-4. Also available in paperback and as an e-book.

> Terry, Sydney, and Jamie—animal friends—go to summer camp and are happy to be in the same cabin. Taylor, a new kid in the cabin, makes hurtful remarks about Jamie and passes them off as jokes. Taylor taunts Jamie for being poor, excludes him, and pulls his friends away from him. Finally, Terry stands up to the bully and tells their counselor what has been happening, restoring her friendship with Jamie. As a consequence, Taylor is moved to another cabin, losing his friendship with Terry and Jamie. The story illustrates the harm that can be done by bullying that is hidden under the pretense of joking and the importance of not being a bystander. K–3.

Frankel, E., & Heaphy, P. (2012). *Weird.* Minneapolis, MN: Free Spirit Publishing, Inc. ISBN# 978-1-57542-398-2.

> Louisa is a spunky girl with her own distinctive style who is made to feel diminished by put-downs from a class bully. After a talk with her mother and some self-reflection, she regains her confidence and the courage to be who she is. The back of the book has several pages of useful tips about how to maintain confidence while being bullied. K–3.

Genhart, M., & Garofoli, V. (2016). *Ouch! moments: When words are used in hurtful ways.* Washington, DC: Magination Press. ISBN# 978-1-4338-1961-2. Also available in paperback.

> The book starts with a couple of examples of physical hurt, such as a bee's sting and catching a finger in a door. After several pages illustrating incidents of words being used in emotionally hurtful ways through taunting, mean jokes, and insults, the book offers children useful strategies for helping themselves and others become more caring and kinder to each other. K–3.

George, Liz. (2016). *Empathy: I know how you feel.* New York, NY: Children's Press (an imprint of Scholastic). ISBN# 978-0-531-21512-8.

> An easy-to-read book that defines empathy and shows children ways to express it to their friends. Illustrated by photos of diverse children expressing a range of emotions, the book also provides strategies and vignettes to practice understanding about the feelings of others. Grades 2–3.

Higgins, M., & Shin, S. (2016). *Teasing isn't funny: What to do about emotional bullying.* North Mankato, MN: Picture Window Books (a Capstone Imprint). ISBN# 978-1-4795-6940-3. Also available in paperback and as an e-book.

> Kelly is a victim of teasing by a small group of classmates (all illustrated as animals). She is insulted on the school bus and in the classroom, until she is befriended by Alex, who comforts her and urges her to tell an adult. The school principal notices that Kelly is upset and encourages her to talk about it. Although Kelly is worried about "tattling," the principal assures her that she is doing the right thing. The principal speaks to the boys who have been doing the teasing and also alerts the school bus driver. Kelly learns to sit up front on the bus near the driver, and she and Alex become friends in school and after school. K–3.
>
> Other books in this series include *Insults Aren't Funny* and *Pushing Isn't Funny.* Each book ends with a glossary, along with suggested Internet sites researched by Picture Window Books staff. They are excellent for introducing various aspects of face-to-face teasing and bullying in grades K–3.

Keller, K. T. (2005). *Courage*. Mankato, MN: Capstone Press. ISBN# 0-7368-3679-9.

> Short, easy-to-read stories, with photographs of diverse young girls performing acts of courage every day, at home, in the community, and at school. Courage is depicted as standing up for a friend, welcoming a new neighbor, owning up to mistakes, and talking to adults about difficult situations. The book also contains stories about a few real heroic women such as Amelia Earhart. K–3.

McCain, B. R., & Leonardo, T. (2001). *Nobody knew what to do.** Morton Grove, IL: Albert Whitman & Company. ISBN# 0-8075-5711-0.

> *Activity #4: Doing the Right Thing

> This is a story of how one child found the courage to do the right thing and tell the teacher about Ray, who was being picked on by a class bully. Together with the teacher and other children who did not want to be bystanders, Ray was befriended and the bully was defeated. The story, about face-to-face bullying and the role of bystanders, is an excellent segue into talking about cyberbullying. K–3.

Penfold, A., & Kaufman, S. (2018). *All are welcome*. New York, NY: Alfred A. Knopf. ISBN# 978-0-525-57964-9. Also available as an e-book.

> A celebration of diversity, this book depicts an early primary classroom with children and teachers representing many different races and ethnicities. The key refrain as children learn, play, and eat together is "All Are Welcome Here." K–3.

Verdick, E., & Heinlen, M. (2004). *Words are not for hurting*. Minneapolis, MN: Free Spirit Publishing. ISBN# 1-57542-156-9.

> A simple exploration of words and the positive or negative feelings they evoke. Clear illustrations of diverse children learning to get along with one another and using their words to solve conflicts and confront teasing. Kindergarten.

Children's Books About Online Safety and Cyberbullying Prevention

Children in grades K–3 engaging in social media is a fairly new phenomenon, albeit one that is growing exponentially. The field of children's literature, especially in the area of picture books, has not kept pace. Generally, books about staying safe online offer good information but are not stories that have emotional impact. Books about cyberbullying also are mostly informational with a few exceptions (mentioned below) that address the emotional issues and harm that surround online victimization.

Caspar, M., & Dorsey, T. (2008). *Abash and the cyber-bully*. Hong Kong and Los Angeles, CA: Evergrow Ltd. ISBN# 978-988-17-3421-1.

> Part of the Emotes! Series, in which each character represents a different emotion, this book features a silly mistake, a digital picture, and a really tough cyberbully. Abash has a very embarrassing day, learns what to do when he feels bullied, and gains empathy for those who do the bullying. The book also contains information about cyberbullying and some helpful hints for children. K–3.

Jakubiak, D. J. (2010). *A smart kid's guide to online bullying*. New York, NY: PowerKids Press. ISBN# 978-1-4042-8114-1.

> This book, part of a series from PowerKids Press, offers simple explanations about many aspects of online bullying. Photographs of diverse preteens and teens illustrate short chapters on topics such as What Is an Online Bully, Why Cyberbullies Bully, Shutting a Cyberbully Down, and Safety Tips. Grades 2–3.

Knowles, C. N. C., & Lewellen, E. (2011). *Piano and Laylee*. Washington, DC, and Eugene, OR: International Society for Technology in Education.

> The Piano and Laylee Learning Adventures series introduces digital citizenship concepts to children ages 5–9. Designed to be read to and shared with early readers, the books follow the adventures of two puppies who learn how to be safe and responsible using technology. They include *Piano and Laylee and the Cyberbully, Piano and Laylee Text*

Message, Piano and Laylee Go Online, and *Piano and Laylee Help a Copycat Become a Creative Cat.* K–3.

MacEachern, R., & Charette, G. (2011). *Cyberbullying: Deal with it and Ctrl Alt Delete it.* Toronto, Canada: James Lorimer & Company Ltd., Publishers. ISBN# 978-1-55277-496-0.

> Cartoon-like drawings are used to define cyberbullying and illustrate the many forms of online bullying, such as calling people bad names, spreading rumors, insulting people, stalking, and threatening. The book also offers a useful list of do-and-don't strategies and helps cyberbullies recognize themselves. Grades 2–3.

Polacco, P. (2012). *Bully.* New York, NY: G. P. Putnam's Sons. ISBN# 978-0-399-25704-9.

> This book is about knowing how to do the right thing. When Lyla moves to a new town before entering 6th grade, she becomes friends with Jamie, who is not popular. However, when she makes the cheerleading team, Lyla has a chance to join the most popular clique of girls. It's fun to be "in" for a while, but when the clique makes fun of Jamie on Facebook, Lyla has the courage to stay true to her friend. *Bully* is a complex story about friendship, cyberbullying, and cheating. Grades 2–3.

Trolley, B. C., Hanel, C., & Shields, L. L. (2009). *Browser the mouse and his Internet adventure.* Chapin, SC: YouthLight, Inc. ISBN# 1-59850-078-3.

> This book tells the story of Browser the Mouse, who makes the decision to try out the new family computer without waiting for his parents' help. His excitement turns to frustration, confusion, and fear as he finds himself lost in a world of chat rooms, blogs, and pop-up windows. After telling his parents everything, they call a family meeting to discuss using technology safely. Designed to promote dialogue and provide practical safety skills for Internet use and cyber balance, the book contains discussion ideas, an Internet safety plan, and a CD with five songs. K–3.

Organizational Resources

Cybersafe Young Children: Teaching Internet Safety and Responsibility, K–3 covers a broad spectrum of issues about good digital citizenship and cyberbullying prevention. For children in grades K–3, ensuring positive social–emotional development and online safety are priority areas of concern. Creating a school culture that fosters kindness, empathy, and respect for differences is a powerful tool to prevent face-to-face bullying—and equally powerful to prevent cyberbullying as children enter the digital age.

Computer lab teachers, children's librarians, and school librarians are important resources for providing high-quality materials such as curricula, apps, picture books, and chapter books that address face-to-face teasing and cyberbullying in developmentally appropriate ways. In addition, many national organizations provide books, blog posts, fact sheets, and other resources for teachers, schools, and parents to help children learn how to navigate the digital world and social media safely and responsibly. A selection of organizations and programs follows.

Children's Safety Network
(childrenssafetynetwork.org)

Children's Safety Network (CSN) is dedicated to many aspects of children's safety, starting in infancy. Bullying prevention is a priority of the organization, and it has produced an interactive webinar, "How Social and Emotional Learning (SEL) Can Help Prevent Bullying," Bullying Prevention Resource Guides, and Bullying Prevention Environmental Scans. A downloadable PDF of the webinar slides is available.

Children's Technology Review
(childrenssoftware.com)

Children's Technology Review (CTR), started in 1993, is an ongoing rubric-driven survey of commercial children's digital media products. Available by paid subscription, the service is dedicated to helping teachers, librarians, publishers, and parents stay up-to-date on new digital products for children ages 0–15. CTR is delivered to subscribers weekly; subscribers also have access to the review database. With the proliferation of apps for young children, CTR is an important source for vetting safety and quality.

Collaborative for Academic, Social, and Emotional Learning (CASEL)
(casel.org)

CASEL is a well-known and trusted source of information about high-quality, evidence-based social and emotional learning (SEL) for pre-K–12 students. SEL competencies include self-awareness, self-management, responsible decisionmaking, relationship skills, and social awareness. CASEL supports school districts, states, and federal policymakers in their efforts to strengthen social–emotional learning as a critical part of education at every level. SEL is a strategy for bullying/cyberbullying prevention.

Committee for Children
(cfchildren.org)

The Committee for Children, founded in 1979, provides advocacy, policy, and evidence-based educational programs to advance the safety and well-being of children through social–emotional learning. One of the committee's signature programs is Second Step, a research-based social–emotional learning program on bullying prevention. Second Step's Bullying Prevention Unit teaches children in grades K–5 how to recognize, report, and refuse bullying. The program also includes online staff training modules.

Common Sense Media
(commonsensemedia.org)

Since 2003, Common Sense Media has been a leading independent source for media recommendations for parents. The organization's education division, commonsense.org/education, has produced a K–12 Digital Citizenship Curriculum in partnership with Project Zero at the Harvard University Graduate School of Education. Free, downloadable lessons for grades K–2, 3–5, 6–8, and 9–12 are available and address such topics as media balance, cyberbullying, online privacy, and news and media literacy. Common Sense Media also reviews and rates apps for children ages 3–16 plus. Criteria include educational value, ease of play, level of violence and scariness, language, and consumerism.

Cyberbullying Research Center
(cyberbullying.org/resources)

The Cyberbullying Research Center is a major provider of research findings, fact sheets, strategies, and resources about a range of cyberbullying issues. The center provides downloadable materials for educators, counselors, parents, law enforcement officers, and other youth-serving professionals. The center publishes timely reports—for example, the 2019 Edition of "Cyberbullying: Identification, Prevention, & Response." It also publishes books on topics related to cyberbullying, including *Words Wound: Delete Cyberbullying and Make Kindness Go Viral* and *School Climate 2.0: Preventing Cyberbullying and Sexting One Classroom at a Time.*

Joan Ganz Cooney Center at Sesame Workshop (joanganzcooneycenter.org/publications)

The Joan Ganz Cooney Center fosters innovation in children's learning through digital media. The organization supports and disseminates research in digital media techniques that advance children's learning. The center publishes industry, policy, and research briefs about key issues in the field of digital media and learning, including "Kids online: A new research agenda for understanding social networking forums" (Grimes, S., & Fields, D., 2012) and "A piece of the puzzle: How media can support the development of empathy, tolerance, and prosocial values in the classroom" (McCain, A. M., & Hilliard, L., 2018).

HITN (hitn.org)

Founded in 1987 as the Hispanic Information Telecommunications Network, HITN works to advance the educational, cultural, and socioeconomic status of U.S. Hispanics. HITN Learning is committed to the social–emotional and academic success of Hispanic/Latinx children ages 0–14 by providing original media learning products in English and Spanish, such as apps, videos, and TV programming. HITN serves learners from diverse cultural backgrounds who value the bilingual English/Spanish experience. HITN is partnering with the Bureau of Youth Diversion and Initiatives at the Brooklyn, New York, District Attorney's office to create "Digital Storytelling" (hitnlearning.org/products/digital-storytelling/), a social-media literacy initiative designed to address the negative effects of cyberbullying.

Massachusetts Aggression Reduction Center (MARC) at Bridgewater State University (vc.bridgew.edu/marc/)

The Massachusetts Aggression Reduction Center (MARC) conducts research and offers anti–bullying/cyberbullying programs to K–12 faculties, administrators, students, parents, and communities in Massachusetts and nationally. The center publishes research reports on a wide range of bullying/cyberbullying issues, such as social-media exploitation and gender-based and peer pressure sexting. MARC has provided evidence-based, low/no-cost programming to more than 400 K–12 schools nationwide over the past decade.

National Association for Media Literacy Education (NAMLE) (namle.net)

NAMLE is a national organization committed to be the leading voice, convener, and resource to foster critical thinking and effective communication for empowered media participation. The organization's vision is to see media literacy as an essential skill for life in the 21st century. NAMLE convenes a biannual Media Literacy conference that is widely attended by teachers, school administrators, parents, and technology experts. A preconference session for early childhood educators brings together thought leaders to discuss how to engage young children in the digital world in developmentally appropriate ways. In 2017, NAMLE partnered with the Technology in Early Childhood Center (TEC) at the Erikson Institute for a one-day symposium titled Media Literacy in Early Childhood: A Critical Conversation. Resources from the symposium are available on the Erikson TEC Center website (padlet.com/tamarakaldor/TECNAMLEResources).

National Association for the Education of Young Children (naeyc.org)

The Fred Rogers Center for Early Learning and Children's Media at Saint Vincent College (fredrogerscenter.org/initiatives/digital-media-learning/resources)

The National Association for the Education of Young Children (NAEYC) and the Fred Rogers Center for Early Learning have worked as a team to advocate for positive, prosocial, and developmentally appropriate practices as children enter the digital world and participate in social media. Developing digital citizenship is at the heart of their joint approach, and they advocate for ongoing research and professional development for early childhood educators. The Fred Rogers Center offers a downloadable list of resources, and it has created a set of mobile apps, ChromaKids, to encourage storytelling (downloadable through iTunes). Children's Technology Review (see p. 81) also is accessed through the NAEYC website.

New America (newamerica.org)

New America is a think and action tank: a civic platform that connects research, technology, media, and the public. The organization works toward a society that promotes economic opportunity for all. Concerning educational policy, New America's program, along with the federal Every Student Succeeds Act, or ESSA (newamerica.org/education-policy/early-elementary-education-policy/early-ed-essa-helping-every-child-succeed), promotes social–emotional learning skills in grades pre-K–3 as important elements of school readiness and healthy child development, which are critical for long-term success in school and in life.

Pacer's National Bullying Prevention Center
(pacer.org/bullying/resources/cyberbullying)

Since 2006, Pacer's National Bullying Prevention Center has been actively leading social change activities to prevent childhood bullying. Pacer works to ensure that all youth are safe and supported in their schools, communities, and online. Pacer reports statistics and trends on face-to-face teasing and cyberbullying, produces case study videos featuring student experiences, and provides strategies for parents. Pacer has recognized that, with the proliferation of young children using technology, parents need information and strategies for protecting their children from cyberbullying.

Pew Research Center
(pewresearch.org/search/cyberbullying)

The Pew Research Center, a subsidiary of the Pew Charitable Trust, is a nonpartisan fact tank that informs the public about the issues, attitudes, and trends shaping the world. Pew publishes reports on a broad range of issues about Internet safety; teens' social media habits, experiences, and behavior; and how parents feel about and manage their teens' online behavior and screen time. The Pew Center provides current and constantly updated data and statistics on young people online.

Power of Zero
(powerof0.org)

The Power of Zero is a global campaign to reshape early learning in the digital age. The program features 12 "Powers for Good" and essays written by well-known early childhood educators on such topics as kindness, critical thinking, inclusivity, and resilience. A division of No Bully, Power of Zero provides families and early educators with books, games, and learning materials to prepare children for living in a digital world. A partnership with Scholastic has produced downloadable K–2 curricula activities about expressing kindness in-person and online (scholastic.com/respect/).

RULER
(ei.yale.edu/ruler/ruler-overview/)

RULER is an evidence-based approach for integrating social and emotional learning into pre-K–12 education. RULER teaches the skills of emotional intelligence—recognizing, understanding, labeling, expressing, and regulating emotions—that are essential to effective teaching and learning. RULER creates safe harbors for children by involving all the adults in the school community, including parents, in training for emotional intelligence. RULER is a national program of the Yale Center for Emotional Intelligence.

Stop Bullying
(stopbullying.gov)

Stop Bullying is a major federally funded government website, providing information and resources to address face-to-face teasing and cyberbullying. Resources cover State Laws and Policies, What Schools Can Do, and What Kids Can Do. The section on cyberbullying is excellent, defining cyberbullying and covering such topics as tactics, prevention, digital awareness for parents, tips for teachers, and how to report incidents.

Technology in Early Childhood Center at Erikson Institute (TEC)
(teccenter.erikson.edu/)

The TEC Center at Erikson Institute offers professional development and an online community for early childhood educators to enhance technology skills and digital media fluency, increase effective use of technology and interactive media with young children, and promote the use of technology in teacher preparation and professional development. TEC advocates for and supports high-quality and developmentally appropriate use of technology and digital media use with young children. The center also believes that, just as early childhood educators foster the development of good citizenship in the classroom, they also need to incorporate good digital citizenship into their curricula as children engage with the online world.

School Statement*

P.S. 321
180 Seventh Avenue, Brooklyn, New York 11215
lphilli@schools.nyc.gov
Elizabeth Phillips, Principal
Beth Handman, Assistant Principal
Sara Despres, Assistant Principal
Elizabeth McCormack, Assistant Principal

DIGITAL CITIZENSHIP AT PS 321

At PS 321, we believe in educating students to be kind, responsible digital citizens and to harness the power of technology for positive uses. We teach all students to code in grades 3–5 and teach students about digital citizenship and safety in all grades. We have a very rich technology program for our upper-grade students. However, over the past few years, we have seen an increase in children's use of various digital devices outside of school (smartphones, tablets, computers, gaming systems) in negative ways. Social networking has become a much bigger part of students' lives at home. As parents navigate the challenges of shaping their children's technology use, we want to share some thoughts and recommendations with you. Although parents of older children probably understand that this handout is relevant to them, we want to urge parents of younger children to take it seriously as well. The earlier parents are aware of some the potential problems of using digital devices, the easier it will be to avoid or minimize some of the problems.

Why Do We Feel So Strongly About This?

Issues that begin online often have deep and lasting effects on students' lives at school. As part of our focus on social–emotional development, we feel it is our duty to share this information with parents. We have seen students who are harassed, bullied, and embarrassed online refuse to attend school, shut down in class, and experience suicidal ideation. Where 5 years ago these were isolated incidents, they have become much more common and occur on an almost weekly basis. We are required by law to investigate these incidents and apply the discipline code as necessary to protect students. This is true even when the incident happens at home if it has an impact on other children who go to PS 321. The investigations can be quite time-consuming and distracting for students and staff. Consequences laid out by the discipline code include revocation of in-school privileges, classroom removal, and sometimes suspension. Students can also face long-term consequences for their missteps online. In recent years, there have been cases of students losing their admission to selective schools when their online behavior was exposed. It can be challenging for adults to fully appreciate the impact that their digital footprint can have; it is so much harder for children, and we need to help them with this.

Parents will make a lot of decisions during the elementary years that will set students' expectations and habits for the future. This is especially true when it comes to their use of technology. In the spirit of collaboration, we are offering some considerations around these decisions:

Think Twice Before Getting Your Child a Smartphone in Elementary School.

Many families get their children smartphones so they can easily reach them when they start walking around the neighborhood more on their own. It doesn't have to be a smartphone. It could be a "dumb" phone or a flip phone—a phone with limited functionality. "Dumb" phones still allow kids to make calls and text. Children can communicate with others without being drawn into the drama that plays out on social media and that they are too young to negotiate. It is much easier to hold off on giving your child a smartphone than to try to take it away if a child misuses it.

Getting kids a smartphone is also such an important decision because with it, they'll have access to all sorts of content despite our best efforts to limit such access. Smartphones are a gateway to a vast world full of content that young eyes shouldn't see (and can't unsee). Just as we don't allow our 4-year-old to watch *The Shining* (the R-rated horror classic) or play *Call of Duty* (an M-rated first-person shooter game), we want to make efforts to prevent our young kids from getting a device that provides endless routes to access developmentally inappropriate content. Plus, there are some unsavory people (e.g., cyberbullies, sexual predators) with whom younger kids will be ill-equipped to deal. Additionally, research indicates that

- The overuse of screens seems to be associated with negative health outcomes, including depression, anxiety, and low self-esteem.
- The relationship between screen use and well-being appears to be bi-directional. For example, kids who are depressed might spend

more time on smartphones/social media and, the more time they spend, the more depressed they get.

- The overuse of screens might be causing negative outcomes by pushing out more need-satisfying activities, which include sleep, physical activity, and in-person social interactions.

Set Limits and Consequences for Phone Use and Screen Time Generally.

Ideally, this is a dialogue between you and your child. If you do decide to give your child a cell phone, it's important to set rules for its use from the beginning. You can say that you're lending them this phone. It's not theirs permanently; you're giving them this phone based on their responsible use of it. If they don't use it responsibly, then they could lose some access. That is considered a logical consequence for misusing the privilege of the phone. Some of those rules should also center around your own access to the device, to ensure your child uses the device responsibly and safely.

Smartphones and smartwatches may never be used during the school day at PS 321. They must remain in backpacks at all times, including at lunch and recess (and out-to-lunch). When setting up ground rules for home, consider setting more restrictions on phone use initially, such as the hours of the day and the places that kids can have it on hand. Many families opt to have a no-phone policy at dinner and in bedrooms to protect sleep and family time. Setting parental controls and keeping passwords protected so children need permission from you to download apps can protect our kids from getting into mature content. It is also a good idea to closely monitor your child's texting and online chats, and their web browsing history. For more information on parental controls, please visit ps321.org/digital-citizenship-safety/

Consider Delaying the Use of Social Media/Social Networking Platforms.

Social networking sites have an age requirement of 13, but many of our students are getting involved with them as young as 8 or 9. In relating to one another, young children inevitably make mistakes and hurt one another, which is part of growing up, but the consequences for these missteps are much greater online because so many more people can see them.

We believe that social networking is harmful for elementary-age students and should be avoided *entirely* until students are older. Elementary school is too early for students to be Instagramming, Snapchatting, and opening themselves up to a world of social interaction where impersonation and public humiliation happen routinely. Many social networking sites also put students in contact with strangers who can misrepresent themselves and pose a danger. If you do allow your children to have social media accounts, please note that they may *never* use their ps321 email addresses to establish these accounts.

Thank you for considering our recommendations. We know that there is a lot of pressure from children to have access to devices earlier and earlier. We encourage you to talk to other parents and think about making agreements about when and how you will allow your children access to devices. We also look forward to discussing this with you in upcoming meetings.

*Reprinted with permission of Elizabeth Phillips and PS 321

Letter from Computer Teacher*

Dear Families,

Throughout the school year, students have been discussing and learning about important digital citizenship issues. Through these discussions, we have discovered that most 4th and 5th graders have unsupervised access to the Internet, and many are sharing personal information and chatting with strangers while playing online games and/or using Social Media apps. We are asking parents to continue conversations with their children about digital responsibilities and online safety. Below are some suggested questions to ask your child, as well as talking points and resources for parents to help facilitate a meaningful discussion around online behavior, safety, and security.

Thank you.

Sara Silver

Computer Teacher

Questions for Parents to Ask Their Kids

1. What do you do when you are online? What games, websites, and apps do you visit?
2. Have you ever gotten an online message or text that has made you feel upset, uncomfortable, or unsafe? What was it?
3. Have you ever chatted online with a person you do not know face-to-face?
4. What have you learned in school about being a good digital citizen and about staying safe online?

Talking Points

- Discuss screen time limits and websites/apps students are allowed/not allowed to use independently.
- Discuss the dangers of online chatting.
- Discuss what private information students should never share online.

Resources

- PS321 Digital Citizenship Page, ps321.org/digital-citizenship-safety/
- Common Sense Media: Parents Need to Know section, commonsensemedia.org
- Common Sense Media: It's Time to Have the Talk, commonsensemedia.org/sites/default/files/uploads/classroom_curriculum/2015_digcit_week_onepager.pdf
- Media Smarts: Guide for Parents, mediasmarts.ca/sites/mediasmarts/files/guides/digital-citizenship-guide.pdf

*Reprinted with permission of Sara Silver

Parent Letter and Questionnaire*

Dear Parents,

As we all are well aware, social media is increasingly available to children at younger and younger ages. I think it is important to address this issue in our class. At our first parent meeting, I look forward to talking with you about how I will be implementing activities this year to help children understand what it means to be a good digital citizen, how they can combat cyberbullying, and also how they can protect themselves online.

As I begin to address these issues, it is important to know about prior experience with digital technology and social media. I have attached a questionnaire about your child's experience with social media online and whether the issue of cyberbullying has come up either at home or at school, prior to this school year.

Thank you in advance for filling out and returning this brief questionnaire. I look forward to your support as I work with your children on what it means to be a good digital citizen.

Yours,

*Adapted with permission of FHI 360

PARENT QUESTIONNAIRE

Please take a few minutes to fill out this questionnaire and . . . (*insert information about how parent should return questionnaire*). Thank you.

Date:

Name (optional):

1. What types of technology does your child use?

2. Do you have family guidelines for the use of technology?

3. Does your child interact online with friends?

4. Do you talk about cyberbullying with your child at home?

5. Has the issue of cyberbullying come up at school?

6. Is there anything else about your child and/or your home use of technology that you would like me to be aware of?

Glossary

App: App is short for "application," a special type of software that can run on an electronic device.

Blog: A place to express ideas and share comments with other people on a special website.

Browser: The system we use to go online and find information.

Cellphone: A phone you can take anywhere.

Chat room: A place on the Internet where people from near and far can talk together at the same time.

Cursor: A little marker that helps you find your place when you are writing online.

Cyberbully: Someone who uses the Internet to say harmful and mean things to another person.

Cyberbullying: Using the Internet to say mean, harmful things to another person.

Cyberspace: The space where online activities happen.

Digital: A coding system using numbers that is like a language for computers.

Download: The way to bring information into your computer from an Internet site.

Email: Notes and messages sent through a computer, a tablet, or a smartphone.

Flip phone: A basic cellphone without Internet access. More compact when closed, the cover "flips open" to reveal the screen, keypad, speaker, and microphone.

Internet: A network that connects computers around the world.

Joystick: The device used to move objects around when playing a computer game.

Laptop: A computer that you can carry around with you.

Log on: The way we sign on to the Internet using a code or password.

Log off: The way we sign off and close down the computer.

Mouse: A hand-controlled device that allows you to point at a particular spot on the computer screen.

Password: A private code you choose to get on to your computer.

Pop-up: A screen that pops up in front of your work without warning.

Search: Finding information online by using key words.

Smartphone: Cellphone that also has Internet access.

Stranger-danger: Harm that can come from talking with and sharing information with someone you don't know.

Surfing: Visiting different Internet sites.

Tablet: A small computer that uses a touchscreen panel.

Texting: Using typed letters to send messages from one cellphone to another.

Website: A connected group of pages on the World Wide Web.

References

Allison, K., & Bussey, K. (2016). Cyber-bystanding in context: A review of the literature on witnesses' responses to cyberbullying. *Children and Youth Services Review, 65*, 13–194.

Alper, M. (2011). Developmentally appropriate New Media Literacies: Supporting cultural competencies and social skills in early childhood education. *Journal of Early Childhood Literacy, 13*(2), 175–196.

Anderson, M. (2018). *A majority of teens have experienced some form of cyberbullying.* Washington, DC: Pew Research Center. Retrieved from pewinternet.org/2018/09/27/a-majority-of-teens-have-experienced-some-form-of-cyberbullying/

Berson, M. J., & Berson, I. R. (2004). Developing thoughtful "Cybercitizens." *Social Studies and the Young Learner, 16*(4), 5–8. Retrieved from hectorsworld.netsafe.org.nz/wp-content/uploads/cybercitizens-ssyl-2004.pdf

Blatchford, P., Pelligrini, A., & Baines, E. (2016). *The child at school: Interactions with peers and teachers.* New York, NY: Routledge.

Bronson, M. (2000). *Self-regulation in early childhood.* New York, NY: Guilford.

Chaudron, C., Di Gioia, R., & Gemo, M. (2015). *Young children (0–8) and digital technology: A qualitative study across Europe.* Luxembourg, European Union, Joint Research Centre. Retrieved from core.ac.uk/download/pdf/159629895.pdf

Children's Internet Protection Act (CIPA). (2011). Washington, DC: Federal Communication Commission. Retrieved from fcc.gov/consumers/guides/childrens-internet-protection-act

Christov-Moore, L., Simpson, E., Coude, G., Grigaityte, K., Iacoboni, M., & Ferrari, F. (2014). Empathy: Gender effects in brain and behavior. *Neuroscience & Behavioral Reviews, 46*(4), 604–627. Retrieved from ncbi.nlm.nih.gov/pmc/articles/PMC5110041/

Committee for Children. (2017). *Bullying prevention in the technology age.* Retrieved from cfchildren.org/wp-content/uploads/policy-advocacy/bullying-prevention-summary.pdf

Common Sense Media. (2013). *Zero to eight: Children's media use in America, 2013.* Retrieved from commonsensemedia.org/research/zero-to-eight-childrens-media-use-in-america-2013

Copeland, W., Wolke, D., Angold, A., & Costello, E. J. (2013). Adult psychiatric outcomes of bullying and being bullied by peers in childhood and adolescence. *Journal of the American Medical Association Psychiatry, 70*(4), 419–426. Retrieved from ncbi.nlm.nih.gov/pmc/articles/PMC3618584/

Copple, C., & Bredekamp, S. (2009). *Developmentally appropriate practice in early childhood programs serving children from birth through age 8* (3rd ed). Washington, DC: National Association for the Education of Young Children.

Cornell, D., & Limber, S. (2016). *Do U.S. laws go far enough to prevent bullying at school?* Retrieved from American Psychological Association, apa.org/monitor/2016/02/ce-corner

Council for the Accreditation of Educator Preparation (CAEP). (2013). *Standard 1: Content and pedagogical knowledge.* Retrieved from caepnet.org/standards/standard-1

Council for Professional Recognition. (2013). *Essentials for working with young children.* Washington, DC: Author.

Cowie, H. (2013). Cyberbullying and its impact on young people's emotional health and well-being. *The Psychiatrist, 37*(5), 167–170. Retrieved from cambridge.org/core/journals/the-psychiatrist/article/cyberbullying-and-its-impact-on-young-peoples-emotional-health-and-wellbeing/B7DB89A2035CF347E73D21EAF8D91214

Dominguez-Hernandez, F., Bonell, L., & Martinez-Gonzalez, A. (2018). A systematic literature review of factors that moderate bystanders' actions in cyberbullying. *Cyberpsychology: Journal of Psychosocial Research on Cyberspace, 12*(4), article 1.

Donohue, C. (Ed.). (2015). *Technology and digital media in the early years: Tools for teaching and learning.* New York, NY: Routledge & NAEYC.

Edwards, S. (2018). Digital play. In R. E. Tremblay, M. Boivin, R. DeV. Peters, & A. Pyle (Eds.), *Encyclopedia on early childhood development* [online]. Retrieved from child-encyclopedia.com/play-based-learning/according-experts/digital-play.

Edwards, S., Nolan, A., Henderson, M., Mantilla, A., Plowman, L., & Skouteris, H. (2018). Young children's everyday concepts of the internet: A platform for cyber-safety education in the early years. *British Journal of Educational Technology, 49*(1), 45–55.

Englander, E. K. (2011). *Research findings: MARC 2011 survey grades 3–12.* Retrieved from Virtual Common, MARC Research Reports (2), vc.bridgew.edu/marc_reports/2

Epstein, A. S. (2009). *Me, you, us: Social-emotional learning in preschool.* Ypsilanti, MI: High Scope Press.

FHI 360. (2016). *Parent survey on use of technology and cyberbullying.* New York, NY: Author.

Flewett, R. S. (2011). Bringing ethnography to a multimodal investigation of early literacy in a digital age. *Qualitative Research, 11*(3), 293–310.

Fluke, S. M. (2016). *Standing up or standing by: Examining the bystander effect in school bullying.* Retrieved from Public Access Theses and Dissertations from the College of Education and Human Sciences, digitalcommons.unl.edu/cehsdiss/26/

Froschl, M., Sprung, B., Mullen-Rindler, N., Stein, N., & Gropper, N. (1998). *Quit it: A teacher's guide on teasing and bullying for use with students in grades K–3.* Washington, DC: National Education Association.

Galinsky, E. (2010). *Mind in the making.* New York, NY: Harper Studio.

Gartrell, D. (2013, March). Democratic life skill 2: Guiding children to express wrong emotions in nonhurting ways. *Young Children, 68*(1), 90.

Grey, A. (2011). Cybersafety in early childhood education. *Australian Journal of Early Childhood, 36*(2), 77–81.

Gropper, N., & Froschl, M. (2000). The role of gender in young children's teasing and bullying behavior. *Equity & Excellence in Education, 33*(1), 49–56.

Guernsey, L. (2014, March 26). *Envisioning a digital age architecture for early education.* Washington, DC: New America Foundation.

Gutnick, A. L., Robb, M., Takeuchi, L., & Kotler, J. (2010). *Always connected: The new digital media habits of young children.* New York, NY: The Joan Ganz Cooney Center at Sesame Workshop.

Hinduja, S. (2018). *Cultivating resilience to prevent bullying and cyberbullying.* Cyberbullying Research Center. Retrieved from cyberbullying.org/cultivating-resilience-prevent-bullying-cyberbullying

Hinduja, S., & Patchin, J. W. (2010). *Sexting: A brief guide for educators and parents.* Cyberbullying Research Center. Retrieved from cyberbullying.org/sexting-a-brief-guide-for-educators-and-parents

John, A., Glendenning, A. C., Marchant, A., Montgomery, P., Stewart, A., Woord, S., Lloyd, K., & Hawton, K. (2018). Self-harm, suicidal behaviours, and cyberbullying in children and young people: Systematic review. *Journal of Medical Internet Research, 20*(4), e129.

Jones, S. (2014). *Examining cyberbullying bystander behavior using a multiple goals perspective: A thesis submitted in partial fulfillment of the requirements for the degree of master of arts in the College of Communication and Information at the University of Kentucky.* Retrieved from uknowledge.uky.edu/cgi/viewcontent.cgi?referer=https://search.yahoo.com/&httpsredir=1&article=1021&context=comm_etds

Lenhart, A., Madden, M., Smith, A., Purcell, K., & Zickuhr, K. (2011). *Teens, kindness and cruelty in social network sites.* Pew Research Center. Retrieved from Pewinternet.org/2011/11/09/teens-kindness-and-cruelty-on-social-network-sites

Lightfoot, C., Cole, M., & Cole, C. (2018). *The development of children* (8th ed.). New York, NY: Worth Publishers.

Linebarger, D. L., Piotrowski, J. T., & Lapierre, M. (2009, November). The relationship between media use and the language and literacy skills of young children: Results from a national parent survey. Paper presented at the annual conference of NAEYC, Washington, DC.

Livingstone, S., Haddon, L., Gorzig, A., & Olafsson, K. (2010). *Risks and safety on the Internet: The perspective of European children.* London School of Economics and Political Science. Retrieved from lse.ac.uk/media%40lse/research/EUKidsOnline/EU%20Kids%20II%20(2009-11)/EUKidsOnlineIIReports/D4FullFindings.pdf_

Mcdonald, N., & Messinger, D. (2011). *The development of empathy: How, when, and why.* Retrieved from researchgate.net/publication/267426505_The_Development_of_Empathy_How_When_and_Why

Mcdonald, N., & Messinger, D. (2011). The development of empathy: How, when, and why. [unpublished paper]. University of Miami, Department of Psychology, Coral Gables, FL.

National Association for the Education of Young Children. (2009). *Developmentally appropriate practice in early childhood programs serving children from birth through age 8: A position statement.* Washington, DC: Author.

National Association for the Education of Young Children & the Fred Rogers Center for Early Learning and Children's Media at Saint Vincent College. (2012). *Technology and interactive media as tools in early childhood programs serving children from birth through age 8.* Retrieved from naeyc.org/sites/default/files/globally-shared/downloads/PDFs/resources/topics/PS_technology_WEB.pdf

National Council of State Legislatures. (2010). *Cyberbullying and the states.* Retrieved from ncsl.org/research/civil-and-criminal-justice/cyberbullying-and-the-states.aspx

National Institutes of Health. (2017). *How does bullying affect health and well-being?* Retrieved from nichd.nih.gov/health/topics/bullying/conditioninfo/health

New York State Department of Education. (2013). *Laws and regulations for Internet safety and cyberbullying.* Retrieved from nysed.gov/edtech/laws-and-regulations-internet-safety-and-cyberbullying_

Olenik-Shemesh, D., Heiman, T., & Eden, S. (2017). Bystanders' behavior in cyberbullying episodes: Active and passive patterns in the context of personal-socio-emotional factors. *Journal of Interpersonal Violence, 32*(1), 23–48.

Olweus, D., Limber, S. P., & Brelvik, K. (2019). Addressing specific forms of bullying: A large scale evaluation of the Olweus bullying prevention program. *International Journal of Bullying Prevention, 1,* 70–84. Retrieved from olweus.sites.clemson.edu/documents/Olweus2019_Article_AddressingSpecificFormsOfBully.pdf

Patchin, J. W. (2016). *Cyberbullying data.* Retrieved from search.yahoo.com/yhs/search?hspart=iba&hsimp=yhs-syn&type=asbw_8063_CHW_US_tid1104&p=Patchin%2C%20J.w.%20%282016%29Cyberbullying%20Data

Plowman, L. (2015). Researching young children's everyday uses of technology in the family home. *Interacting with Computers, 27*(1), 36–46.

Poole, C., Miller, S., & Church, E. (2019). *Ages and stages: Empathy: How to nurture this important gateway to social and emotional growth.* Scholastic. Retrieved from scholastic.com/teachers/articles/teaching-content/ages-stages-empathy

Ragozzino, K., & Utne O'Brien, M. (2009). *Social and emotional learning and bullying prevention.* Education Development Center. Retrieved from promoteprevent.org/sites/www.promoteprevent.org/files/resources/SELBullying%281%29.pdf

Reflection Sciences. (2018). *Executive function & social development: What's the connection?* Retrieved from reflectionsciences.com/social-development

Schweinhart, L. J., Barnes, H. V., & Weikart, D. P. (1993). *Significant benefits: The HighScope Perry preschool study through age 27.* Monographs of the HighScope Educational Research Foundation, 10. Ypsilanti, MI: HighScope Press.

Second Step. (2018). *The power to create a positive school climate.* Seattle, WA: Author. Retrieved from secondstep.org/bullying-prevention#research-materials-section

Soyeon, K., Scott, R., Colwell, K., Boyle, M., & Georgiades, K. (2018). Cyberbullying victimization and adolescent mental health: Evidence of differential effects by sex and mental health problem type. *Journal of Youth and Adolescence, 47*(3), 661–672.

U.S. Department of Education. (2016). *Early learning and educational technology policy brief.* Retrieved from tech.ed.gov/earlylearning/

Vygotsky, L. S. (1987). Problems of general psychology. In R. W. Reiber & A. Carton (Eds.), *The collected works of L. S. Vygotsky* (Vol. 1). New York, NY: Plenum.

Index

About the Authors

Barbara Sprung, Merle Froschl, and Nancy Gropper have been leaders in the field of equity-based early childhood materials since the early 1980s. They have collaborated on books, articles, and curriculum on emerging issues such as nonsexist early childhood education, supporting boys' learning, and addressing "face-to-face" teasing and bullying behavior in grades pre-K–3. They co-authored *Supporting Boys' Learning: Strategies for Teacher Practice, Pre-K–Grade 3*, published by Teachers College Press in 2010. They also have taught a blended seven-session course on the subject for Bank Street College in 2013/2014. In 1978, Froschl and Sprung were the project directors and Gropper the research director and evaluator for a groundbreaking project that resulted in the publication of *Quit It! A Teacher's Guide on Teasing and Bullying for Use with Students in Grades K–3*. Gropper and Froschl also co-authored "The Role of Gender in Teasing and Bullying Behavior," published in *Equity & Excellence in Education* (2000) and presented a paper on the topic at the 1999 AERA conference in Montreal, Canada. Over the years, their work has been supported by the U.S. Department of Education, the National Science Foundation, The Carnegie Corporation, The New York Community Trust, and many local and national foundations and corporations.

Barbara Sprung, now retired, was co-director of Educational Equity at FHI 360. She has over 40 years of experience in early childhood education as a teacher and as an innovator of programs and materials to promote equality of opportunity for children regardless of gender, race/ethnicity, disability, or level of family income. Projects include Right from the Start in the Digital Age, Raising and Educating Healthy Boys, Great Science for Girls, Science: It's a Girl Thing!, and After-School Math PLUS.

From 1982 to 2004, Ms. Sprung was co-founder and co-director of Educational Equity Concepts, a national nonprofit organization whose mission was to create bias-free programs and materials beginning in early childhood. Ms. Sprung has written extensively about equity in education and is a nationally known speaker on issues of gender equity, teasing and bullying, early science equity, and inclusion. She is the author of *Non-Sexist Education for Young Children: A Practical Guide* (1975), editor of

Perspectives on Non-Sexist Education (Teachers College Press, 1978), a co-author of *Quit It! A Teacher's Guide for Use with Students in Grades K–3* (1998), the *Anti–Teasing Bullying and Teasing Book for Preschool Classrooms* (2005), and *Supporting Boys' Learning: Strategies for Teacher Practice, Pre-K–Grade 3* (Teachers College Press, 2010).

Ms. Sprung holds a BA degree from Sarah Lawrence College and an MS in child development from the Bank Street College of Education, and she is a graduate of the Institute for Not-for-Profit Management, Columbia University. In 2011, she was a recipient of the Bank Street College Alumni Award. In 2016, she received the Willystine Goodsell award for gender equity from the Women's Special Interest Group at the American Education Research Association.

Merle Froschl is director of educational equity at FHI 360, where she provides leadership and oversight to projects that include curriculum development, professional development, parent education, research, and evaluation. Ms. Froschl has over 35 years of extensive experience in developing innovative programs and materials that foster equality of opportunity for students regardless of gender, race/ethnicity, disability, or level of family income. She was the co-founder and co-director of Educational Equity Concepts, Inc., a national nonprofit organization whose mission was to create bias-free programs and materials.

Since the 1980s, Ms. Froschl has developed outstanding curricular and teacher training models in the field of educational equity and is a nationally known speaker on issues of gender equity and equality of opportunity in education. She is the co-author of *Quit It! A Teacher's Guide for Use with Students in Grades K–3* (1998), the *Anti–Teasing Bullying and Teasing Book for Preschool Classrooms* (2005), *Supporting Boys' Learning: Strategies for Teacher Practice, Pre-K–Grade 3* (Teachers College Press, 2010), and "Improving Boys' Achievement in Early Childhood and Primary Education," in *Lessons in Educational Equality* (2012).

Merle Froschl holds a BS degree from Syracuse University and is a graduate of the Institute for Not-for-Profit Management, Columbia University. In 2016, she received the Willystine Goodsell Award for gender equity from the Women and Research in Education Special Interest Group at the American Education Research Association.

Nancy Gropper, now retired, began her career in early childhood education more than 50 years ago as a teacher of young children. She moved on to higher education as a member of the teacher education faculty at Brooklyn College and at the State University of New York at New Paltz, where she served as chair of the Department of Elementary Education. More recently she was a member of the graduate faculty at Bank Street College, where she served as director of student teaching, chair of the Department of General Teacher Education, and associate dean in the Graduate School of Education.

Dr. Gropper's professional endeavors—conference presentations, workshops, and publications—have focused on issues affecting the education of young children. Her doctoral dissertation explored young children's understanding of gender with a seminal early publication co-authored in the *Harvard Educational Review* titled "Sex Role Culture and Educational Practice" (1974). In recent years, she has co-authored *Supporting Boys' Learning: Strategies for Teacher Practice, Pre-K–Grade 3* (Teachers College Press, 2010) with Merle Froschl and Barbara Sprung. She also joined with Nancy Balaban to co-author the 5th and 6th editions of *Observing and Recording the Behavior of Young Children* (Teachers College Press), a book that was originally published in 1958 and authored by Dorothy H. Cohen and Virginia Stern.

Dr. Gropper holds a bachelor's degree in child development from the University of Delaware and a master's degree and a doctorate in early childhood education from Teachers College, Columbia University.

Printed and bound by CPI Group (UK) Ltd, Croydon, CR0 4YY

16/04/2025